# *the*
# PRAYING
# FAMILY

CREATIVE
WAYS
TO PRAY
TOGETHER

*the*

# PRAYING
# FAMILY

# KIM BUTTS

Praise Covenant Church
3501 S. Orchard
Tacoma, WA 98466

MOODY PUBLISHERS
CHICAGO

Scripture taken from the *Holy Bible, New International Version*®. NIV®. Copyright ©
1973, 1978, 1984 by International Bible Society. Used by permission of Zondervan
Publishing House. All rights reserved.

Library of Congress Cataloging-in-Publication Data

Butts, Kim, 1954-
    The praying family : creative ways to pray together / Kim Butts.
        p. cm.
    ISBN 0-8024-3086-4
        1. Family--Religious life. 2. Family--Religious aspects--Christianity.
    3. Prayer--Christianity. I. Title.

BV4526.3 .B88 2003
249--dc21

                                                    2002013016


1 3 5 7 9 10 8 6 4 2

*Printed in the United States of America*

*I dedicate this book to my Father in heaven,*
*who wants all men everywhere to lift up holy hands in prayer.*
*May it bring honor and glory to His name*
*as families learn to seek His face together in prayer.*

# Contents

| | | |
|---|---|---|
| | Foreword | 9 |
| | Acknowledgments | 11 |
| | Preparing for Family Prayer | 13 |

**Part 1: Beginning to Pray Together**

| | | |
|---|---|---|
| Journey #1 | Becoming a Lighthouse of Prayer | 32 |

**Part 2: How Do We Pray?**

| | | |
|---|---|---|
| Journey #2 | Praying the Word of God | 52 |
| Journey #3 | I'm Sorry, God | 64 |
| Journey #4 | Prayers of Thanksgiving and Praise | 82 |
| Journey #5 | The Anytime and Anywhere of Prayer | 98 |
| Journey #6 | Prayer Commands in Scripture | 120 |

**Part 3: Praying for Others**

| | | |
|---|---|---|
| Journey #7 | The Needs of Others | 146 |
| Journey #8 | Our Ten Most Wanted | 154 |
| Journey #9 | Prayer Missionaries | 164 |
| Journey #10 | Putting Feet to Your Prayers (Prayerwalking) | 180 |

**Part 4: Special Types of Prayer**

| | | |
|---|---|---|
| Journey #11 | Prayer Parties | 192 |
| Journey #12 | The Family Blessing | 224 |
| | Conclusion | 236 |
| | Prayer Journey Resources | 238 |

# Foreword

Are you almost frantically looking for a way to insulate your children from the escalating evil in our country?

Do you worry about the incessant vying for their minds by producers of lewd and violent movies, videos, Web sites, CDs and electronic games? Does your heart almost despair at the words of their music and the lies and deceit saturating their world and even sometimes taught in their schools?

Are you longing to instill in them an unshakable faith in God that will see them through any future terrorist attacks or wars? To so ground them in who God is that, no matter what lies ahead that would rob them of their security, He will be One to whom they will automatically turn?

Also, are you desperately trying to change your neighborhood for the better, but feel you are failing miserably? Would you like *your* home to be the one to which others would run in case of a family crisis or natural disaster, but feel you don't qualify?

Take heart. There is an answer to your fears and longings—contained right in the book you are holding in your hands. It is called *family praying.*

This book is an incredibly complete resource on family praying that will inspire you and challenge you to start what you may have been missing—or to launch you into experimenting with surprising new methods and journeys of prayer.

After a lifetime of prayer ministry, I found myself propelled ever onward, waiting to see what was coming next!

It also wisely contains the changes in your family God requires before you can become effective in praying for and reaching the lost in your neighborhood with Jesus. Their accepting Jesus one by one is the only fool-proof way of actually transforming your neighbors.

Take a quick quiz with me. What percentage of your personal and family time per week do you spend listening to human input on a horizontal earthly level? Now, what percentage do you spend communicating vertically with the God of the Universe? Are you shocked at the ratio—and at how little time you actually are spending as a family talking to and listening to God?

If so, this book is for you—just brimming with practical, do-able, attainable biblical models and methods to fit all stages of spiritual maturity, all levels of prayer expertise, and all ages from toddlers to grandparents. Pick those that fit your individual family right now—and get ready for the journey of your life.

Evelyn Christenson

# Acknowledgments

It has been a privilege to have the opportunity to develop a prayer tool to put into the hands of families. My passion for the past several years has been teaching parents, grandparents, Sunday school teachers, and others to teach children to pray. Many of these people kept saying, "We don't know how to pray . . . how can we teach our children?" They didn't feel they had enough of a handle on their own prayer lives to confidently guide and train their families in prayer. So when the offer came to write a book on praying families, I was eager to move forward with a project near to my heart.

How grateful I am to the Lord for the patient understanding and encouragement of my husband, Dave. I know that I was able to complete this project because he has been faithful to pray for me and with me, day by day. Thanks, Dave. You are the epitome of Ephesians 5:25–28, and you have taught me that prayer is the primary divine activity God has called His people to engage in during our short time on this earth. I look forward to many more years of fruitful ministry with you as He provides.

I also want to thank our youngest son, David, who, because of being homeschooled, has been actively connected to this project from the beginning. Thank you, Son, for being patient throughout this process, for learning the fine art of cooking frozen pizza and rolled tacos, for letting me talk about you in the book, and for always providing comic relief when I need it. Thanks go as well to our adult son, Ron, who always has the assurance that he is prayed for daily no matter where he is: We know that the Lord has amazing plans ahead for you!

I have been blessed by several brothers and sisters in Christ for their generous contributions to this book and want to extend them thanks.

To *Al VanderGriend,* Lighthouse Coordinator for Mission America, for his encouragement, for pioneering the wonderful prayer evangelistic tool of Lighthouses of Prayer, and for allowing me to freely use his material. Praying the Five Blessings for our neighbors and friends has been a blessing in the life of my family! (See Journey #1: Becoming a Lighthouse of Prayer.)

To *Kyle and Kathy Harris,* missionaries to Papua New Guinea with Pioneer Bible Translators, for their purposeful adaptation of the Five Blessings prayer for missionaries. (See Journey #9: Prayer Missionaries.)

To *Steve Hawthorne,* for his passion for the lost, and for generously allowing me to adapt material from *Seek God for the City,* a forty-day prayer guide seeking God for spiritual awakening in our cities and communities.

To *Jan Wade-Littrup* for her wonderful inspiration and insights into Prayer Parties, and for her generous spirit in sharing them with me!

To *Elsa Mazon, Dave DeWit,* and *Anne Scherich* of Moody Press, for their help in bringing this book into publication.

To *my fellow workers at Harvest Prayer Ministries* who have been so understanding about the time it has taken to do this project. They have prayed for me and encouraged me continually.

To *all of my friends and family* who have prayed earnestly for me for months! Don't stop now!

# Preparing for Family Prayer

Since my earliest memories of simple prayers at the family dinner table, the Lord has graciously led me on my own personal journey of prayer day by day. As I learn more about the character of Jesus and grow deeper in my walk of faith, my prayer life is stretching and growing in ways I never would have imagined. When Dave and I began Harvest Prayer Ministries in 1993, we never dreamed what God had in store for us. He has faithfully revealed more of His heart to us as we have daily sought to seek His face and draw closer to Him. As we began to actively involve our family in the journey of prayer, we learned together about His faithfulness.

Family prayer in our household has been a series of wonderful successes tempered by some total failures. We have rejoiced in the victories, as our faith was strengthened. We have learned from and grown significantly from the things that haven't worked well. Sometimes my husband and I have felt like Jehoshaphat, who prayed in 2 Chronicles 20:12, "We do not know what to do, but our eyes are upon you." Our patient, loving Father took us step-by-step, as He will also do for you. The disciples asked Jesus to teach them to pray, and He did. We need only to ask, and He will teach us.

## HUSBANDS AND WIVES

If I could encourage parents in any one area as you lead your families into journeys of prayer, it would be this: Pray together regularly! My husband and I have made it a daily practice to pray together as husband and wife. (If you are a single parent, find at least one prayer partner who has children and covenant with one another to pray for each other and for your children.) No other spiritual practice has impacted my life as much as this one, outside of my own personal devotions.

If you as a couple pray together, don't keep it a secret. Mentor others by sharing your experiences in prayer. Can you imagine the impact within your church if you would encourage other couples (especially newlyweds) to pray together as husband and wife? It is not difficult to see the impact this would have on our families.

Dave and I have had so many precious times of praying back and forth, lifting one another up before the Lord. How comforting it is to hear my husband asking His blessing on each activity of my day. What a privilege to be able to do the same for him.

## THE EXAMPLE OF PRAYING PARENTS

A woman who attended one of my seminars told me that she remembered walking by her mother's bedroom door, which was left ajar, and hearing her name mentioned. "It made me feel so good," she said, "to hear my mother talking to God about me." I rejoice as I listen to David pray, knowing that he has grown up with prayer as an integral part of his life and in our life as a family. He knows without doubt that the Lord hears and answers prayer, and it is part of who he is as a Christian.

Family prayer has taken on different forms in our household throughout the years, to grow and change with our sons; however, it has always been front and center. If you ask both boys (who are over nine years apart in age) which family night of ours they remember the most, it was the one that ended with a prayer time involving the different postures of prayer. Dave read Scriptures that described how different people in the Bible prayed, and then we all spent some time praying that way. We knelt, we stood up and lifted our hands before the Lord, and we even lay on our faces together. Of course, we all laughed a lot, as we felt a bit self-conscious doing this together —but we all would say that it gave us a new freedom in the way we pray.

If you are interrupted for some reason on this journey of family prayer, get back at it as soon as possible. Persevere, knowing that Jesus has the victory in prayer. "Consider it pure joy, my brothers, whenever you face trials of many kinds, because you know that the testing of your faith develops perseverance. Perseverance must finish its work so that you may be mature and complete, not lacking anything" (James 1:2–4). It will be a day-by-day kind of journey, but the end result will be a lifetime of answered prayer and a greater understanding of the heart of God. Best of all, you will have children who pray and are committed to seeking His plan and purpose for their lives.

## JOURNEY GUIDELINES

When most families go on a journey, whether it's vacation or a weekend trip, they do several things: They plan and talk about where they will go and what they will do; they make preparations ahead of time; and they anxiously await the adventure that lies ahead. It is my prayer that *The Praying Family* will provide an unforgettable series of fun and creative prayer journeys for your family and that your personal and corporate prayer lives will be transformed.

Each journey your family takes will teach a concept about prayer. Some journeys are very simple; others more complex. Some will take longer than others. You can skip all around the book if you wish, depending upon what seems appropriate and interesting to your family. Pick and choose your activities, just like you would select items from an à la carte menu. It is even possible to be on two journeys at the same time.

Please know that *The Praying Family* is intended to meet the needs of your family. Be as flexible as you wish and as creative as you want to be.

### Prayer à la Carte

Each journey is broken up into "steps" instead of days. Different journeys will take different amounts of time, and your family will determine how long that will be. You have the flexibility to determine the amount of time you will spend on a particular step or journey. There is something to fit every family's schedule.

Remember, this is a smorgasbord of prayer! You can repeat steps of a journey or incorporate different parts of several journeys into one. The versatility of this format will allow you to have family prayer experiences together for years to come. The first time you take a journey, travel "in order" to learn the concept more thoroughly. Much will depend upon the ages of your children and the difficulty of certain steps. Feel free to add, subtract, or adapt as needed. Adding steps from other journeys can help enhance your experience as you travel and learn together.

### Family Involvement

These journeys are meant to involve everyone—from youngest to oldest—in a cooperative effort. Allow all of your children to take an active part in every step. If you have children with special needs, either mental or physical, adapt these journeys in whatever way is necessary for their active participation. The more fun you have and the more hands-on involvement your children have, the deeper the concepts of prayer will sink in and become a part of who you are as a family and as individuals.

### Preparing Your Hearts

The goal is not to complete these journeys but to focus on the person of Jesus Christ and to learn how to pray what is on His heart. That will mean lining up what *you* want with what *He* wants. One way to do this is to take some time each day to worship the Lord as a family. Read a passage of the Psalms or sing a song of praise together before you begin. Get your minds focused on the Lord first—then on the journey.

### Choosing a Journey

Choose journeys you think your family will be most inter-ested in as you begin. You can take more difficult journeys based on ages of your children and as your family matures in prayer. Journeys can be shorter and slower for beginners, or longer and more fast paced for those who wish to move at a more advanced level. Parents—you need to read through each journey ahead of time so that you will be able to pick and choose what is best for your family's needs.

### Preventing Information Overload

Many times it is easy to be paralyzed into inactivity when there are too many choices or too much information. If you are like me, you can easily go into "overload." Don't allow all of the information found in this book to overwhelm you. Take things one step at a time and have fun! Be cautious about trying to do too much too fast. Relax and enjoy whatever pace your family may take on a given journey. Sometimes it will be fast and furious; other times it will seem to take a long time to finish a journey. Allow the Holy Spirit to be your guide and your teacher. If one journey isn't working for your family, try another one. Perhaps you will be ready to come back to the former one at a later time.

## *Journey Journals*

Journey Journals are optional, but I strongly encourage you to use them. You can purchase or make your own "empty books" to use as journals. The Journey Journal can be used as a kind of diary. Write the name of each journey you take at the top of a page. Keep track of the dates, as it will be a good experience to go back and look at some of the things you have done and how you have grown in prayer. Write down what you are learning and your thoughts, feelings, and special memories. For young children, try to have a journal without lines so that they can easily draw pictures of their experiences.

## *Side Trips*

Side Trips are provided to give variety and to allow families to pick and choose activities that will interest and involve children of different ages. They are relevant to the concepts being taught and reinforce what is being learned. You may even wish to interrupt the steps of your journey with a Side Trip, especially if you have very young children.

Side Trips are also good for individual family members

who wish to dig deeper along the journey and have some additional adventures. Sometimes the entire family may not have time to take a particular Side Trip. Encourage children to take a Side Trip on their own from time to time. Have them report back to the family what God is showing them.

## Memory Verses

Each journey will have at least one Memory Verse for your family to learn. Younger children may use a shorter version of verses that are quite long, but you will be surprised at how good these young ones are at memorization. Review your Scriptures regularly to retain them. God's Word should always be a lamp to your feet and a light for your path (Psalm 119:105).

## How to Make This a Journey for a Lifetime

How to Make This a Journey for a Lifetime sections close the journeys and reinforce prayer concepts and release your family into prayer ministry. They are meant to help you sustain interest and continue to grow after you have taken the initial journey. If you catch a vision for what God would like to do in and through you as you pray, you will be able to make each learning experience a Journey for a Lifetime.

## Resources

At the end of the book, you will find a resource section with books, tools, videos, and Web sites that might be helpful to your family. It will be useful to look through this section before you take a journey to see what resources you could use to enhance your adventure in prayer!

**Praise Covenant Church
3501 S. Orchard
Tacoma, WA 98466**

## SPECIAL TIMES OF FAMILY PRAYER

Pray together each time you meet. Don't leave out this most important element—even in the interest of time. During the day, if the opportunity presents itself, join with one or more family members to pray. Wouldn't it always be great to know that your family is lifting you up in prayer whenever you need it?

Don't get so busy learning about prayer together that you don't pray as individuals. Encourage one another to have personal prayer time and study each day. These journeys are not meant to take the place of each family member's individual quiet time with the Lord. Our personal journeys with God take place in our own prayer closets as we seek His face. (See Journey #5, "The Anytime and Anywhere of Prayer.")

## OVERCOMING OBSTACLES

This book is useful for families that are just beginning to learn to pray and for families that are spiritually mature in this area. Satan will, almost without exception, put up roadblocks when it comes to praying together as a family. I have listed some of these obstacles so that you can be aware of them ahead of time. I have also tried to give ways to overcome each obstacle. As you do so, you will be free to make prayer the most fun and effective activity you do together as a family.

### The Parental Prayer-Ability Factor

"How can I teach my children to pray when I don't do it well myself?" Many parents feel inadequate to teach their children to pray. This book is set up to encourage families to *pray together* and to *learn together* as they begin to develop strong lifetime habits in effective praying. Because parents and kids are learning concepts on the same level, parents don't have to feel the pressure to be a prayer expert. They simply need to follow through and reinforce what is learned in the context of family prayer experiences from day to day.

Still, it is vitally important that parents are godly examples of praying people for their children. As your children see and hear you praying, they will pray. Develop your prayer life continually. Teach and train your children as they grow in knowledge and wisdom of the Lord (Proverbs 22:6; Joel 1:3). Children should always obey and respect their parents (Ephesians 6:1–3; Colossians 3:20).

### The Time Factor

Many parents balk at beginning any kind of family devotions or spiritual training because they lack enough time to prepare or can't see how the family can find the time in everyone's hectic schedules to do the lesson. However, the prayer journeys in this book involve limited time in preparation. Needed materials can usually be found around the house or easily made. Schedules are often the biggest hurdle. If your family can only squeeze in fifteen minutes at a time, you can still learn and reinforce valuable concepts and pray together. Do what you *can*, not what you can't.

### The Guilt Factor

Parents usually feel guilty because they don't have enough time or feel they don't pray well enough. One simple fact will release you from this: Guilt does not come from God—it comes from the Enemy! If you are feeling guilty about your prayer life, you are letting Satan beat up on you! The Enemy doesn't want families praying together and will do anything he can do to discourage you, because he knows he is defeated in prayer. Purpose to become a praying person, and a praying parent or grandparent, and ask the Lord to guide and direct you. Then place your prayer life into His capable hands, rejoicing about what He will do in and through you, and leave the guilt behind!

### The Boredom Factor

Usually this is on the part of the kids but can also be a problem with parents when their prayer experiences have been less than fulfilling. Many feel that prayer seems like inactivity. This book is designed to provide stimulating and different ways to pray, so that prayer can become the most exciting activity a family engages in together. Your enthusiasm will help to spark excitement in your children. Look at these journeys as thrilling adventures in communicating with the Lord of the universe!

### The "Getting Teenagers to 'Buy In'" Factor

For older children to get actively involved, they have to "buy into" the purposes and plans God has for His people as they pray. Study the Scriptures listed below with them ahead of time (consider it a kind of pre-journey) and discuss why it is important for your family to become a praying family.

1. *Jesus tells us to pray and gives us many instructions!* And do you know what? These are not just prayer suggestions—they are prayer commands from the very heart of God. Read the following Scriptures together:

   • Matthew 6:5–8: Jesus says, "*When* you pray" . . . not "*if*" you pray.

- Matthew 5:43–45; Luke 6:27: We are to pray for those who persecute us.

- Matthew 26:41: We need to pray so that we do not fall into temptation.

2. *Jesus modeled prayer for us continually when He walked on this earth.* He gave us His example and instruction on how to pray. Read the following Scriptures together:

- Luke 11:1–4: The disciples only asked Jesus to teach them one thing: how to pray . . . and He did.

- Luke 6:12–13: Jesus spent the night in prayer, apparently asking God for wisdom and discernment. The next morning, He chose His twelve apostles.

- Luke 9:28: Jesus took Peter, John, and James on a prayerwalk up a mountain; read what happened next.

- Mark 1:35: Jesus prayed in solitary places, early in the morning.

- Matthew 14:23: Sometimes Jesus prayed when He was tired from ministering to so many people and needed to spend some time alone with His Father.

- Luke 22:41–44: Jesus prayed during the most difficult circumstance in His life and submitted Himself to the will of God.

3. *Jesus continues to intercede for us today.* Read the following Scriptures together:

- Romans 8:34: Jesus does not condemn us but intercedes for us.

- Hebrews 7:25: Jesus is the holy and blameless High Priest who prays for us continuously.

4. *Many other Scriptures give us direction in prayer.* Read the following Scriptures together:

- Ephesians 6:18; Jude 1:20: We are to pray in the Spirit and keep on praying for the saints.

- 1 Thessalonians 5:17–18: We are to pray continually, giving thanks in all circumstances, because it is God's will for us.

- James 5:13: We are to pray when we are in trouble.

- James 5:16: We are to confess our sins to each other and pray for each other so that we may be healed.

- 1 Peter 4:7: We are to be clear minded and self-controlled so that we can pray.

- 1 Timothy 2:1–4: God desires us to pray for those in authority . . . because He wants everyone to be saved and to come to a knowledge of His truth!

## The "Cute" Factor

Please, please, please understand that children are not "practicing" when they pray. They are vitally needed as prayer warriors in this dark, lost world! If parents, pastors, and youth workers take the position that the prayers of little children are just "cute" rather than powerful and effective (which is how God hears them), we are a lot like the disciples at the early stage of their ministry. In their ignorance, they attempted to discourage those who brought children to Jesus. Read Mark 10:13–16. Jesus knew that God has placed tender, unpretentious hearts in children and that they come before the Father honestly and earnestly —believing! Too often, we have looked at our children as the church of tomorrow. My friend Vicki Murello, children's pastor at our church, refers to our children as "The Church of *Now!*"

We must not quell their natural interest and desire to pray. Once my husband and I were teaching about prayer and evangelism to a group of kindergarten students. After we had finished, we asked if one of the children would like to pray. Many times the kids will get really shy all of a sudden or pray so quietly that no one else can hear (which is OK, since it's really only important that God hears). However, on this particular occasion, a little girl threw her hand up in the air, almost bursting with her desire to be the one to pray. When she began, she stood up on a chair, threw her shoulders back, and belted out one of the most glorious, God-honoring prayers I've ever heard! We were weeping when she finished, as she had truly prayed out of the very depths of her heart for the lost. Obviously, she had been encouraged in her young prayer life by her parents and, at her very tender age, knew the power of prayer and the Lord who answers prayer. If we had prayed, or asked another adult to pray instead, we would all have missed a powerful and precious blessing.

Several years ago, I witnessed a very wise mother as she encouraged her young daughter (probably about three years of age at the time) to pray before bedtime. Without hesitation, Michaela looked around her room and thanked God for everything she could see—including her curtains and her Barbie dolls. My friend Anita could have said something like, "Honey, let's find some new things to pray about—I don't think God really cares very much about every little thing in your room." Do you think this little girl would have opened her mouth in prayer the next night? I don't. Her exuberant little spirit would have been crushed and replaced by uncertainty in a desire to please her mother, rather than God.

Instead, her mother wisely said, "Honey, that was a great prayer! I'm sure God is so pleased that you are such a thankful little girl! Let's spend a little bit of time praying for our family tonight too, OK?" She then proceeded to pray for other family members, which Michaela picked up on quickly and joined in. This mother did two important things: She recognized the validity and importance of her little one's prayer before God, and she modeled a way for her child to stretch and grow in prayer.

Children need to be taught to realize that God has expectations for them. Look at Proverbs 20:11; 1 Timothy 4:12; Jeremiah 1:7–8. Youth and inexperience do not matter to God. When He chooses to call someone—young or old—He equips and prepares them. Throughout the Bible, we see a picture of children praising and interceding—even being called to fast (Psalms 8:2; 148:7–13; Joel 2:15–16; Matthew 21:14–16).

Never assume that children are too young to grow in their understanding of prayer. You will not only be doing a disservice to them but to yourself—and to God, who wants to use them! I have often been asked how early children can be introduced to the concept of prayer. My response is that children should be exposed to prayer and encouraged to pray as early as possible.

I had to experience this to believe it myself. Little Marissa, only eighteen months old at the time, was taking a nap when we came to have supper at her house. When she woke up, we were well into the meal with her parents and older sister. Her mother put her in her high chair, placed her dinner in front of her, and we went on with our conversation.

It became apparent quickly that Marissa was not eating and was upset with us. When her mother asked her what was wrong, she held both arms out to her sides and bowed her little head in a gesture that said, "My meal hasn't been blessed yet."

Sheepishly, we all joined hands and prayed a blessing over the food again, and Marissa happily began to eat. Prayer was not a ritual for her—it was a lifestyle. You will rejoice together as you see even the youngest child coming boldly before the throne of God in earnest, heartfelt prayer.

### The Difficulty Factor

Don't make prayer harder than it is—prayer is simply talking with God. As long as your family knows that prayer is not a difficult thing and sees it as exciting, it will become a natural part of who you are as a family.

### The Pride Factor

Parents do not have to be the "prayer experts." You just need be willing to learn together *with* your children. Sometimes one or both parents will need to overcome the "pride factor" and be willing to learn from even the youngest children, as you seek to know God's heart in prayer.

### The "Oh No, I Don't Want to Pray Out Loud" Factor

Praying out loud is a big roadblock for many people—especially adults and teenagers. So, if one or more family members need to pray silently for a while in order to feel comfortable, then do that! God is perfectly capable of hearing all of our prayers, whether they are out loud or silent. Never pressure someone who is uncomfortable praying out loud but continue to encourage him or her to try.

Why is it important to pray out loud? The Bible says that Christians are to pray individually *and* corporately. Praying out loud also helps you to pray in agreement with one another.

When one person prays about a person or issue, someone else may also wish to add a prayer about the same topic. When you pray out loud, others can be blessed or encouraged. Here is an easy way to take children (adults can do this too) through the process of learning to pray out loud:

> *Praying Scripture out loud to the Lord:* Choose a psalm like Psalm 145 and pray it back to the Lord.
>
> *Echo Prayers:* One person says a short sentence prayer— the next person "echoes" it.
>
> *Fill in the blank:* Lord, thank You for _____; or, Lord, I praise You for _____.
>
> *Sentence prayers:* Echoed first; then try a short one alone.
>
> *Know whom you are talking to:* Talk to God without worrying about what others think—learn to talk to Him from your heart, just like you were praying silently. He is your heavenly Father who loves you! Your prayers are not directed to your family members— they are directed to God alone!
>
> *Empty-Chair Prayer:* Put an empty chair next to you when you pray. Imagine that Jesus is sitting in the chair and you are having a conversation.

### FINAL PREPARATIONS

Now that you are aware of the potential obstacles and how to overcome them, you will want to spend some time in prayer dealing with any roadblocks that stand between your family and an exciting adventure of prayer. When you feel satisfied that your family has dealt with all of the issues mentioned above, it is time to go on your first journey together.

I pray that through the guidance of the Holy Spirit these concepts will touch your hearts in a way that will allow Christ to lead each individual and your family as a whole toward a lifestyle of powerful, purposeful prayer. It is also my fervent hope that prayer will be woven into the very fabric of your family's life—from youngest to oldest—as you bring your hearts into alignment with the power and plan of God and as you learn to pray what is on His heart. May your family be known by friends, family, neighbors, coworkers, schoolmates, and others as a family that prays! And, may it be not only life changing—but catching!

PART 1

# BEGINNING
# TO PRAY
# TOGETHER

# Becoming a Lighthouse of Prayer

*What Is a Lighthouse?*
*A Lighthouse is a family or a group*
*of two or more people who gather together*
*to pray for, care about, and share Christ*
*with their neighbors.*

❧

*There is nothing that makes us love a man so*
*much as praying for him.*

WILLIAM LAW

What could God do in the lives of your neighbors if your family would pray for them? We have had many new opportunities to speak with our neighbors and to minister God's love to them since we started praying for them. Stories from friends of ours, as well as stories from all over the world, have convinced me that being a Lighthouse of Prayer is one of God's strategies for reaching the lost. Lives are changing, people are coming to Christ, families are being restored, relationships are being healed . . . because neighbors have been praying for neighbors.

## WHAT YOUR FAMILY WILL DISCOVER ON THIS JOURNEY

➤ *How to pray effectively for the people who live in your neighborhood*

➤ *How lives can be changed forever as you pray for your neighbors to come to know Christ and have opportunities to care for them and share Jesus with them*

➤ *How God can do awesome things in the lives of people in your neighborhood and draw them to Himself through your family's prayers*

➤ *How praying for people helps you love them like Jesus loves them*

## ⏱ PREPARATION TIME:

Just as getting in shape for physical journeys is important, so it is a good idea to get in shape spiritually before a spiritual journey. The journey to become a Lighthouse of Prayer involves the spiritual *and* the physical! Spend time together as a family praying that the Lord will use you in powerful ways to help transform the lives of many neighbors as you pray for them, care for and about them, and share Jesus with them in meaningful ways.

## ▤ MATERIALS NEEDED:

⟿ A concordance, preferably an exhaustive concordance for the version of the Bible your family uses, although the concordance in the back of a Bible will be fine

⟿ A Bible for each member of the family

⟿ Journey Journals (optional)

⟿ Lighthouse of Prayer materials (optional) (see Resources)

## ▲ SIDE TRIPS:

Don't forget to check the Side Trips available to you! There will be at least one or two that will apply to each step of your journey.

Some Side Trips are more suited to younger children, whereas others will appeal to the older members of the family. Keep this in mind as you plan and prepare everyone ahead of time—especially if you are going to take a Side Trip geared toward little kids. Teens need to know that some days the trips will be on a younger level, whereas other days they will be a big stretch for the little ones.

Try to keep this as even as you possibly can if this is an issue in your family. Remind your children that the purpose is to learn *together* about prayer. Also, *individual* family members can take Side Trips without the entire family going along—and report back to everyone at the start of the next day of a journey. Ask for volunteers to go on certain Side Trips and share what they have learned. This could be a good solution for older children when you wish to take a Side Trip geared toward younger children.

 MEMORY VERSE:

*John 8:12*

**STEP ONE**   📖 Practice your memory verse

➔ *Preparing a prayer map*

Draw a map of your neighborhood or apartment complex, putting some kind of identifying mark on the houses of the five neighbors you are going to pray for on this journey. (If you wish to pray for more than five neighbors, please do!)

You can simply write the last name of each family on the map or assign a different color to those houses or apartments that represent your "prayer targets." Younger children can draw pictures of each family inside their houses. Keep this map in a place where everyone can refer to it (on the refrigerator is often a good place). It will be a good daily reminder to pray. Begin to pray that God will draw your neighbors to Himself and that He will use your family in a powerful way.

**STEP TWO** 📖 Practice your memory verse

➲ *Gathering information*

If you can, learn the names of the people in each home and any other information that will help you as you pray. Together, write down in your Journey Journals as much about each family as you can.

- Are there children in this home? If so, what are their names? What grades are they in?
- Where do the parents work and the children go to school?
- Does the family have any needs you know about?
- Do they have a personal relationship with Jesus?

Other information is great, but you don't want to be nosey! As you get to know these neighbors better, you can gradually add information to your journals so that you can pray more effectively and specifically for them.

**STEP THREE** 📖 Practice your memory verse

➲ *Making a Lighthouse of Prayer window poster*

Make your own Lighthouse of Prayer window poster to use during this journey. You can put it in your window to let people know that your house is a Lighthouse. Draw a colorful lighthouse and write on it: "Our House Is a Lighthouse of Prayer." You may also want to make some cards or door hangers to leave for the neighbors you are praying for. These can be very simple and just say that your family is praying for theirs.

Work on these cards as you have time so that they will be ready when you want to use them.

If you don't have time to make the materials, you can order any Lighthouse of Prayer materials you will be using—window decals to identify your home as a Lighthouse, door hangers, greeting cards, and other items. There are also some special pamphlets and booklets to help you. (See Resources for all of these.) Your neighbors will eventually identify you as the family that prays.

## STEP FOUR  📖 Practice your memory verse

➲ *Preparing in prayer*

Spend some time in prayer together. You can use the prayers given here, if you wish, or you can pray your own prayers. It is very important to remember that the most important need of your unsaved neighbors is to recognize their sinful condition and their need to accept Jesus Christ as Savior and Lord. When you pray for them using Scripture, you will need to be careful not to pray prayers that are intended for Christians. Some blessings cannot come to unbelievers until they come to Christ.

**Read:** John 6:44

**Pray:** "Lord, help our neighbors to be drawn to You as we pray."

**Read:** Psalm 51:10

**Pray:** "Lord, reveal anything in *our lives* that could keep our prayers for our neighbors from being effective."

**Read:** Romans 6:23

**Pray:** "Father, prepare the hearts of our unsaved neighbors to clearly see the sinfulness that separates them from You."

**Read:** 1 Timothy 4:12; Philippians 2:14–16a

**Pray:** "Lord, help us to be good examples of Jesus to our neighbors."

How about a Side Trip?

**STEP FIVE** 📖 Practice your memory verse
➲ *"The Five Blessings"*

Now that you have prepared physically and spiritually and know which neighbors you will pray for as a family, you are ready to begin praying for them. Pray for each of the five families you have chosen in your neighborhood. Bring each family's name before the Lord, using individual names as you feel led.

As a family, make a commitment to pray for your five families five minutes a day, five days a week, for at least five weeks, using the five blessings that are described below. These blessings correspond to the letters of the word *bless:* Body, Labor, Emotional, Social, and Spiritual.

The Five Blessings method of praying is adapted from material written by Dr. Alvin VanderGriend, Lighthouse Coordinator for Mission America.

Write this down in your Journey Journals so you will remember:

Pray for five families . . .
  • Five minutes a day

  • Five days a week

  • For five weeks

Pray the Five Blessings:
  • **B—Body** (physical needs)

- **L—Labor** (school or work)
- **E—Emotional** (thoughts, feelings)
- **S—Social** (relationships—friends, family)
- **S—Spiritual** (coming to know Christ or getting to know Christ better)

**STEP SIX**    📖 Practice your memory verse

➲ *"The Five Blessings": B—Body*

**Pray** for your neighbors' physical bodies and needs for their health, safety, and well-being.

**Read:** Matthew 6:33

**Pray** that they may seek the kingdom of God first and receive all other blessings they need as well.

➲ *"The Five Blessings": L—Labor*

**Pray** for your neighbors' labor (work) or for children or young adults who are students, their studies, and that they will do well in school.

**Read:** Proverbs 10:4

**Pray** that your neighbors' hands will always be diligent (busy at work) and never lazy.

➲ *"The Five Blessings": E—Emotional*

**Pray** that your neighbors' emotional needs will be met by knowing Jesus, so that they will live peaceful lives, and will experience joy and happiness.

**Read:** Proverbs 1:33

**Pray** that your unsaved neighbors will listen to God and

receive Christ as Lord and Savior, so that they may experience
His promised blessings: "Whoever listens to me will live in
safety and be at ease, without fear of harm."

⊃ *"The Five Blessings": S—Social*

**Pray** for your neighbors' social needs—friendships and
family relationships.
**Read:** Malachi 4:6
**Pray** that your unsaved neighbor families will turn to God
in right relationship so that they will be able to relate to one another in a godly way.
**Read:** Luke 10:25–37
**Pray** that your unsaved neighbors will learn to love the
Lord with all of their heart, soul, strength and mind. Pray that
they will follow Christ, and love their neighbors (including
you) as themselves. Pray also that God will give your family
this same love!

⊃ *"The Five Blessings": S—Spiritual*

**Pray** that those who do not know Christ will sense their
need for Him and begin asking the right questions; pray that
those who *do* know Christ will be strengthened in their walk
with Him.
**Read:** Acts 16:14
**Pray** that people's hearts will be open to believe.

**Read:** Acts 17:27
**Pray** that the unsaved persons you name before God will
seek Him, reach out to Him, and find Him, since "he is not far
from each one of us."

**STEP SEVEN** 📖 Say your memory verse
Pray the Five Blessings for your five neighborhood families

➲ *Scripture search: B—Body*

**Find** Scriptures that you can use to pray for "Body" and write them in your Journey Journal. If you can't find any Scriptures of your own, try these: Psalms 104:14; 145:15–16; Matthew 6:26; James 1:17.

**Write** short prayers for your neighbors, using each verse. Pray that the members of each family will have good health, that the Lord would keep them safe from harm, and that those who have physical or mental disabilities will be healed. Now you will have lots of fresh prayers to pray each day for the physical well-being of your neighbors.

**Pray:** "Lord, if there is any way that You want to use me (us) to be the answer(s) to my (our) own prayers, please show me (us)."

**Journey Journals:** Be ready to write in your Journey Journals as you become aware of how God is answering your prayers for your neighbors.

**Younger Children:** Have younger children draw pictures in their Journey Journals about one or two of the Scriptures.


**STEP EIGHT** 📖 Say your memory verse
Pray the Five Blessings for your five neighborhood families

➲ *Scripture Search: L—Labor*

**Find** Scriptures for "L—Labor." Here are some suggestions: Proverbs 10:4–5; 14:23; 27:18; Ecclesiastes 5:12.

**Write** a short prayer for each verse. Don't forget to write at least some of these prayers down in your Journey Journal so that you can pray with some variety. Pray that your families will work hard in school or at work, that they will get along with fellow workers and fellow students and teachers, and that they will respect those who have authority over them.

**Pray:** Ask God to open doors for you to take the next step with your neighbors—showing them sincere Christian love.

**Don't forget** to thank God for each of your neighbors and to pray that God will use you to be the answer to some of your prayers for them.

**Journey Journals:** Remember to write in your Journey Journals as God answers prayers.

**Younger Children:** Have younger children draw pictures in their Journey Journals about one or two of the Scriptures.

Remember the Side Trips!


**STEP NINE**   📖 Say your memory verse
Pray the Five Blessings for your five neighborhood families

   ➲ *Scripture search: E—Emotional needs*


**Find** additional Scriptures for "E—Emotional needs." Here are some suggestions: Psalms 42:5; 34:14; 1 Peter 5:6–7.

**Write** prayers in your Journey Journals using these Scriptures.

**Pray** that your neighbors' family members will have their emotional needs met, will feel good about themselves, and will be content in their circumstances. Pray that God will bring them caring friends to listen to them.

**Don't forget** to thank God for each of your neighbors and to pray that God will use you to be the answer to some of your prayers for them.

**Journey Journals:** Don't forget to write in your Journey Journals as God answers prayer.

**Younger Children:** Have younger children draw pictures in their Journey Journals about one or two of the Scriptures.

## STEP TEN 📖 Say your memory verse
Pray the Five Blessings for your five neighborhood families

➲ *Scripture search: S—Social needs*

**Find** additional Scriptures for "S—Social needs." Here are some suggestions: Proverbs 17:17; 18:24; 22:6; Ecclesiastes 4:10; Hebrews 13:4.

**Write** short prayers for each Scripture verse.

**Pray** that the parents in your neighbor families will be loving to their children, that the children will be obedient to their parents, that individuals in the family will have caring, close, healthy relationships with their friends and be kind to one another and to others.

**Don't forget** to thank God for each of your neighbors and to pray that God will use you to be the answer to some of your prayers for them.

**Journey Journals:** Don't forget to write in your Journey Journals as God answers prayer.

**Younger Children:** Have younger children draw pictures about one or two of the Scriptures in their Journey Journals.

Today would be a great day for a Side Trip!

## STEP ELEVEN 📖 Say your memory verse
Pray the Five Blessings for your five neighborhood families

➲ *Scripture search: S—Spiritual needs*

**Using your Bibles,** find additional Scriptures for "S— Spiritual needs." Here are some suggestions: Psalm 34:8; Isaiah

55:6–7; Acts 2:21; 26:18; Romans 2:4; 10:9; 2 Corinthians 4:4; Hebrews 11:6.

**Write** short prayers for several of these Scriptures that you can pray for your neighbors.

**Pray** that your neighbors will be convicted of sin, come to a saving knowledge of the truth, and will accept Jesus as Savior and Lord.

**Don't forget** to thank God for each of your neighbors and pray that God will use you to be the answer to some of your prayers for them.

**Journey Journals:** Remember to write in your Journey Journals as God answers prayer.

**Younger Children:** Have younger children draw pictures in their Journey Journals about one or two of the Scriptures.

## 🌲 Side Trips

### ➲ Making a lighthouse

Tell everything you know about real lighthouses. What do they do? What do they look like? Look up additional information, if you want. Discuss how this Lighthouse Journey (praying for your neighbors) makes your family similar to a real lighthouse. Have the younger children draw a picture of your family as a Lighthouse.

### ➲ Sending out cards and letters

• Once a week for five weeks send a note or Prayer-A-Gram (see Resources) to the neighbors you are praying for, letting them know that you are praying for them. Start today. If you continue to pray after the five weeks, send a note once a month. You can alternate with prayer poems that share the message you are praying.

• See Resources for more information about obtaining Prayer-A-Grams, greeting cards, "I Said a Prayer," and other prayer poems that can be enclosed in a note or left at a neighbor's home.

• Younger children can draw pictures to be included in the notes or can dictate a message to be written by an older child or parent. There are also some wonderful greeting cards available from HOPE Ministries. (See Resources.) These will announce that you are praying for your neighbors.

➲ *Scripture study: "God puts the 'light' in lighthouses"*

Using a concordance, study all of the Scriptures that talk about *light*. There are several good ways to do this (choose one):

• Take the time to go through the Scriptures on *light* using a concordance. Discuss how these Scriptures apply to you as a family.

• Assign each person several Scripture passages to look up. Each person should take turns sharing with the rest of the family what he has learned about light. Discuss how these Scriptures apply to your family.

• Have one family member "sort out" the Scriptures on light that can specifically relate to being a lighthouse. Assign one or more verses to each family member to read. Discuss how the Scriptures apply to your family.

• Pray about how God can use you to be a light in your neighborhood. Ask Him to make you a light as individuals and as a family to those you are praying for specifically.

After studying the Scriptures on light:
- Remember to write down in your Journey Journal some of the Scriptures on light that are meaningful to you.

- Younger children can illustrate some of the Scriptures.

## *Special Side Trips for very young prayers:*

Even the youngest child can participate in being a Lighthouse. Have young children join in as many of the above-mentioned activities and Side Trips as possible. Give them specific things to pray about and give them special jobs, such as helping to send or deliver notes. Share prayer requests from the neighborhood and also share the answered prayer stories with them. Make sure they share answered prayers that they become aware of. Don't forget that the prayers of even the youngest person in your family are just as important as those of anyone else!

### ➲ *Take a ride on "Reminder Railroad"*

Have the young children draw pictures of lighthouses for each member of the family to remind them that your family is a Lighthouse of Prayer. Hang the pictures in the bedrooms, in the car, or on the bathroom mirror.

### ➲ *Go to "Need-a-Light Cavern"*

Have the children meet with you in a dark place or wait until night and turn out the lights. Talk about how those who don't know Jesus are living in darkness. Shine a flashlight or light a candle to represent a lighthouse in the midst of darkness. Share with them how Jesus can shine through your family in a dark place to bring light because of your prayers.

## ➲ *Visit "Two-Palm Island"*

• Set up a small prayer box in your front yard. It can be an actual mailbox, although you will want to place it off the street a bit and away from other mailboxes to avoid confusing your mail carrier.

• Write "Prayer Requests" on both sides of the box—large enough to be seen from across the street.

• Pass out fliers to your neighbors with a letter identifying your family as desiring to be a Lighthouse in your neighborhood. Let them know that if anyone has a need that they would like to have your family pray about, they can write it down on paper (or you can provide special note cards) and drop it in your prayer box. Let them know that the requests can be anonymous or they can identify themselves—whichever they prefer. All you ask in return is that they share answered prayer with your family—or put another note in the prayer box when the prayer is answered.

Here is a sample letter:

Dear Neighbors,
Our family, as believers in Jesus Christ, has committed together to pray for our neighbors on a regular basis because we care very much about each and every one of you. We are already praying daily for you, but if you have a specific request that you would like us to pray, please put a note in the box marked "Prayer Requests" located in our yard. The only thing we would like from you is that you let us know when you have an answered prayer in your life or in the life of your family.
   May God bless you and keep you,
   The Smith Family (Don, Cathy, Jamie, and Sarah)
   5555 S. Maple Ave.

Another good way to let people know you are praying is to use greeting cards or a door hanger (see Resources).

### ➲ Go to a "Lighthouse Luau"

Have a special celebration as God answers your prayers in the lives of your neighbors. Be sure to give God all the glory and praise for what He is doing in their lives.

Point out to children that answered prayer does not have anything to do with our efforts. Instead, the prayers are answered as we are simply obedient and as God works in and through us to change the lives of others.

Take turns thanking God for what He has done!

You might plan a special celebration meal to share together.

### ➲ Dig for gems in "Question Quarry"

Ask the following questions:

• What is the most important thing I (we) have learned about light?

• What would happen in this nation if thousands of families like yours became Lighthouses of Prayer?

• Do our prayers make a difference in the lives of our neighbors? How?

⤳

## HOW TO MAKE THIS
## A JOURNEY FOR A LIFETIME

1. Continue this journey as the Lord leads. Add new neighbors, rejoice over those who come to Christ and/or experience answers to prayer, and continue to let your neighbors know that you are praying for them.

After several weeks, begin to do "random acts of kindness" for your neighbors, such as taking cookies or fresh bread over, raking their yards or picking up trash, or helping out when they have a need. They will begin to see the love of Jesus shining in you, and they will all know that you pray for them.

2. Pray that God will provide opportunities for your family to share Christ in tangible ways with your neighbors.

3. Tell other Christians about being a Lighthouse of Prayer so that this nation will be saturated with the light of believers praying blessing into their neighborhoods. Maybe your own church would like to become a Lighthouse for the community around it!

4. Begin to pray for other neighbors—and for unsaved friends and family. Stretch beyond your "five-neighbor" limit. Pray until you see results for every family. (Know that this could take years—but God is in control.)

5. Write down the answered prayers to encourage yourself and your family, as well as to encourage your neighbors.

6. Continually pray, believing that God is going to do amazing things in response to your family's prayers.

PART 2

# HOW DO
# WE PRAY?

# Praying the Word of God

*The child learns to speak
because his father speaks to him.
He learns the speech of his father.
So we learn to speak to God because
God has spoken to us and speaks to us.
By means of the speech of the Father in heaven
His children learn to speak with Him.
Repeating God's own words after Him,
we begin to pray to Him.*

DIETRICH BONHOEFFER

Learning to pray Scripture—communicating with God in His own words—has revolutionized the way I pray. It leads me into intimate worship and communion with God. It gives me a fresh, new, and exciting vocabulary to express my heart to the Lord. Best of all, I am starting to hear the Word of God come freely out of my mouth as I pray, which means that it is becoming part of me!

Praying God's Word into the lives and situations of others is an authoritative way to pray His will for them. The Lord said that His Word will not return to Him empty but will accomplish what He desires and achieve the purpose for which He sent it (Isaiah 55:11). For example, right now I am praying a special Scripture for my teenager. It is from 1 Timothy 4:12:

> Father, please don't let anyone look down on David because he is young but help him to set an example for believers and unbelievers in his speech, in his life, in his love, in his faith, and in his purity.

For my husband, I am praying a passage from Jeremiah 17:7–8:

> Lord, please bless my husband, because he is a man who trusts in You and places his confidence in You. May he be like a tree planted by water that

sends out its roots by the stream. Help him not to fear when the heat comes. May he always be productive for You. Help him to have no worries, and may he never fail to bear fruit in the ministry You have given him.

Do you see how praying the Word into someone's life can make a powerful difference? When you pray the Word of God into a life or a situation, you will be able to pray with the confidence that you are *always* praying in His perfect will.

## WHAT YOUR FAMILY WILL DISCOVER ON THIS JOURNEY

➤ *Prayer is simply talking with God*

➤ *This two-way conversation involves* listening—*you will discover how to hear God's voice more clearly as you become more familiar with it*

➤ *Exploring God's Word in prayer helps you discover a powerful, wonderful way to communicate with God, a way that pleases Him greatly and will help your entire family to be excited about the possibilities of prayer*

➤ *Praying the Word of God gives you an expanded prayer vocabulary that goes beyond anything you may have ever thought to pray before*

➤ *You can break out of a "prayer rut" and never experience that problem again*

➤ *Getting to know Jesus better helps you grow in your love for Him*

## 🗏 MATERIALS NEEDED:

- ➲ Bibles
- ➲ Concordance (optional)
- ➲ Journey Journals (optional)
- ➲ Paper
- ➲ Card file box and 3 x 5 cards
- ➲ Pens or pencils (crayons or markers for younger children)
- ➲ Dry-erase board or a chalkboard (helpful but not necessary)
- ➲ Thesaurus (helpful—especially when trying to define words so that the younger children can understand)

## 📖 MEMORY VERSE:

*Luke 11:28*

**STEP ONE** 📖 Practice your memory verse
   ➲ *Listing some of God's attributes and character traits*

**Choose** one person to be your "scribe." The scribe will keep track of your journey on paper.

**Read:** Psalm 145. Focus on the attributes and character of God.

Working together, make a list of all the attributes and character traits you can find in Psalm 145. (Parents might wish to change some words to make them easier to understand.) Write these traits and characteristics on a dry-erase board or chalk-board or have one person make the list so that everyone can see it. Next, look to see if your list is something like the one started below. (Please note, if yours is different, it's *not* wrong! It's important that it be an expression of your family's communication with the Lord, not an exact replica of mine. This is just an example of how yours could look.)

> God is the King!
> He is worthy to be praised and exalted (glorified) every day!
> He is so great that no one can fathom (understand) the
>     depth and extent (amount) of His greatness!
> His acts are mighty!
> His majesty is glorious and splendid!
> (Finish the rest of the psalm.)

Spend a few minutes in prayer together. Choose one attribute (characteristic, part) of God and thank Him: "Lord, thank You for Your mighty acts! Father, we thank You that You are the King!" Let everyone who wishes to have a turn to pray out loud do so.

**STEP TWO**  📖 Practice your memory verse
  ➲ *Praising God for His attributes*

Take turns choosing different attributes (qualities) of God from the list you made in Step One of your journey. Spend some time praising God out loud from His own Word! For example: "Lord, we give You praise because Your majesty is glorious and splendid!" (If praying out loud is uncomfortable for one or more, please be reassured that God is perfectly able to hear our praises even when they are quiet.) Isn't it wonderful to have such a variety to choose from and such special ways to praise Him? What other words can you think of to describe what God is like?

➲ *Rewriting a psalm*

Together, rewrite Psalm 145, or another of your choosing, changing the pronouns to focus on the Lord. For example, when the psalm reads, "The Lord," you can put in the pronoun "You." If you wish, you can leave the psalm in the first person or change it to reflect your family (change "I" to "we"). When you read it over, your rewritten psalm should sound as though you are reading it to the Lord. If you need some help, see if your version looks similar to the one started below (remember, your rewritten psalm should reflect your family and doesn't have to be exactly like this one):

We will exalt (pay tribute to) You, our God the King. Every day we will praise You and extol (worship) Your name for ever and ever. Lord, You are so great and most worthy of praise; Your greatness no one can fathom (understand). May our generations share Your works with other generations to come. We will tell of Your mighty acts. Lord, we will speak of the glorious splendor of Your majesty. We will meditate on Your wonderful works . . .

**Ask:** Do you realize that we have written a prayer of praise to the Lord?

**Choose** one person in your family to read this prayer to the Lord as you pray together.

**Say:** We have just communicated to and communed with God in His own words!

**STEP THREE** 📖 Say your memory verse

➲ *Saying prayers of thanksgiving*

**Read:** Psalm 145

**Choose** one person to read this short example from Psalm 145:

> Thank You, Lord, for being gracious and compassionate, slow to anger, and rich in love! Father, we are so grateful that You are faithful to all of Your promises and that You are so loving toward us. Thank You for lifting us up when we fall and for giving us our food and satisfying our desires. Knowing that You are near to us whenever we call upon You in truth is such a blessing—thank You! We give thanks that You watch over us!

**Choose** a different family member to pray the following prayer—this time from Psalm 95:

> Thank You, Lord, for being the Rock of our Salvation, the great God, the great King above all gods. We give You thanks for being our Maker and because we are the people of Your pasture, the flock under Your care!

**Remember:** If you have very young children in your family, you may wish to change some wording so that it is easier to understand. Here is an example:

> Thank You, Lord, for being like a rock that we can always count on and for being the Rock that saves us! Thank You that there is no other god—only You! Thank You for making us and for taking care of us! . . .

**Share** with your family that praying prayers of thanksgiving from God's Word is *very* scriptural. Have someone read Ephesians 5:19–20 out loud.

**Say:** After we "practice" praying His Word in this way, we will have a larger vocabulary with which to thank Him for all He has done, is doing, and will continue to do in and through our family.

**Note:** The "practice" is still very valid prayer that is heard by God! Please don't allow anyone in the family to think that these prayers will only be for "real" when you have practiced for a while. We become better pray-ers by spending time in prayer. God is listening and is pleased by every effort we make!

## STEP FOUR 📖 Say your memory verse

Here are some questions to discuss today. I suggest that you have your Bibles and Journey Journals handy if you are using them. Give everyone a chance to participate:

**Ask:**
- What have you learned about the character of God? (What is God like?)

- What are some of His attributes (qualities) that you had never really thought about before?

- Do you feel that praying in this way will help you to understand God better? Why?

- Will praying in this way help you to expand your own personal prayer life? How?

- Do you think God is pleased when we communicate with Him using His own words? Why?

- How can God speak to you through His Word and/or in other ways as you focus on Him?

**Say:** Now we know how to describe God, praise Him, and thank Him in some new ways. Let's try praying together, using some of what we have learned! Remember: God wants to hear what is on your heart and my heart too. Praying God's words as well as our own draws our hearts together as we line up our requests with His will.

**Listen:** Spend some time quietly listening and allowing God to speak to your hearts.

**Pray:** "Thank You, Lord, that Your Word is a lamp to our feet and a light for our path" (Psalm 119:105).

## STEP FIVE 📖 Say your memory verse

➲ *More words to describe God*

**Say:** Let's find another psalm, part of a psalm, or another passage in God's Word that offers up praise to Him and teaches us about His character and qualities.

**Activity:** Have different family members look up one or more of these suggestions from the Psalms: Psalms 29:1–4; 93; 95:1–7; 103; 146:6–10.

**Read:** Take turns reading these passages.

**Share:** Tell what new words you have learned to describe God from these passages. Write them in your Journey Journals.

**Pray:** Spend some time together in prayer. Try using some new words from God's Word!

## 🌲 *Side Trips*

➲ *"My sheep know my voice"*

Make a short tape recording of the voices of each person in the family. Have them talk in their natural voices, then in quiet voices, loud voices, and in a whisper. Mix the voices up, keeping track of which family member is at what place on the tape. Play the voices, seeing if the others can recognize who it is. This is a good way to illustrate how well we can come to know God's voice by spending time with Him in His Word and in prayer. The more we spend time listening to a voice, the better we know it, whether it is loud, soft, normal, or in just a whisper.

Make another tape. This time, record different family members and friends all saying the same sentence. Somewhere in the middle, put in a voice that is unfamiliar. Play the tape and have everyone write down the names of the persons whose voices they hear. They should leave a blank for any they can't get (it will probably be only the unfamiliar voice you have placed in the middle). This is another way to teach them that we learn the voices of those we are close to. We should get to know God's voice as easily as the voice of someone in the family.

### ➲ Prayer picnic

Plan a picnic together. Decide where you'll go, pack a lunch, think of all of the details—lawn chairs, blanket, bug spray, sunscreen, hats. On your way, write down all of the things you see that remind you of God. Or draw pictures! Share as you go! Then, before you sit down together to enjoy your picnic, your prayers will be filled with thanks and praise.

### ➲ "God Is"

Using colorful markers or crayons and strips of paper, write one attribute of God each day to put in a central place (table, refrigerator, kitchen island). See how many days you can do this by continuing to look for new descriptions of God. Take turns. You can write something like this: "God is _____." When you have written all the words you can think of, take the papers out, throw out any repeats, and count how many you have! Spread them out on a table and pray, praising God for who He is!

### ⮞ *Scripture gifts*

Find one passage of Scripture for each family member. Write a prayer for each person based on that Scripture. Put it into your Journey Journal to remind yourself to pray. Then write the Scriptures on pieces of paper or on cards and give them to each person. This will be an encouragement to each person in your family as the others commit to praying God's Word over them.

⁂

## HOW TO MAKE THIS
## A JOURNEY FOR A LIFETIME

1. Whenever you read Scripture, write down words that describe God or tell about Him. Keep a card file that you can review often as you pray. It is a fun way to use fresh, new phrases and words to praise God with as you pray. Pretty soon, these words and phrases will become a natural part of your prayer life.

2. Do word studies on words that describe God. For example: *awesome*. There are at least twenty-five references to our awesome Lord! Use a concordance to find some of them. Keep them in your file! Some of these phrases would be powerful additions to your prayer life.

3. Try writing down some of the prayers that the Lord places on your heart. Fill them with many words of praise and thanks. Pray them out loud to God; write a

poem or a song. Share them with other members of your family or with friends.

4. Each day when you wake up, think upon the wonderful descriptions of God—before you even get out of bed!

5. Whenever you come across a Scripture that reminds you about another person and what he is going through right now, write it down and pray that as a prayer for him. You can let him know what you are praying if you feel led to—it might be a real encouragement for him at just the right time.

# I'm Sorry, God

*For I will forgive their wickedness*
*and will remember their sins no more.*

HEBREWS 8:12

Our family has learned some very important lessons about sin, confession, repentance, grace, and forgiveness over the years. We homeschool and travel a lot as a family. Being with each other so much and often in close quarters can cause us to do and say things we shouldn't. We've found out that quickly asking for forgiveness after an angry or hurtful word is said draws us closer together than ever. If there is no resolution to the situation, the hurt or anger can grow and become more harmful.

Confessing our sins to God and to one another, repenting (being sorry and saying so), and either asking for or giving forgiveness are crucial to our relationships. It is important to humble ourselves enough to say, "I'm sorry" to God and to the person who has been hurt so that things can be made right between us and God and between family members. Also, it's much more fun to be in a right relationship to one another and to God than to waste time in self-pity or being stubborn about apologizing.

If your family is like ours, most of the disagreements are over small things that don't really matter much unless they are not dealt with quickly. Then little sins can grow larger and more serious. God has given us His grace so that we can forgive as He forgives us. Life is too short to waste His time by holding on to sinful behavior or unforgiveness. My husband calls it

"Keeping short accounts with God." Scripture describes how love allows us to forgive and forget the wrongs that have been done to us by the power of love that God has placed in our hearts for our family:

> Love is patient, love is kind. It does not envy, it does not boast, it is not proud. It is not rude, it is not self-seeking, it is not easily angered, it keeps no record of wrongs. Love does not delight in evil but rejoices with the truth. It always protects, always trusts, always hopes, always perseveres. (1 Corinthians 13:4–7)

Most important, pray together after you have had a disagreement or said something hurtful. After you have dealt with the sin and asked for or given forgiveness, prayer will restore you to fellowship with one another and to God. This is crucial, whether it is between husband and wife, parent and child, or sibling and sibling. Then, God can be free to pour out His grace to allow us to begin again—fresh and new!

> Bear with each other and forgive whatever grievances you may have against one another. Forgive as the Lord forgave you. And over all these virtues put on love, which binds them all together in perfect unity. (Colossians 3:13–14)

## WHAT YOUR FAMILY WILL DISCOVER ON THIS JOURNEY

> ❧ *What the Bible has to say about sin, confession, repentance, grace, and forgiveness; sin confessed with a repentant heart and a determination to change our behavior brings forgiveness through God's grace*

➢ A very important part of prayer is how to keep "short accounts" with God so that He will hear and answer

➢ It is important to confess sin before coming to the Lord in prayer

➢ God will forgive us as we forgive others

## ⏱ PREPARATION:

Words to know

**Sin**—Sin is anything that causes us to be disobedient to God. When we disobey God our sin makes Him sad. It can make other people sad too. We can be disobedient in several ways:

• By doing or saying something that goes against God's Word. Usually this will do some kind of damage to another person—physically, emotionally, or spiritually (Exodus 20:12–17; Mark 9:42; Romans 13:8–10).

• By doing or saying something against God Himself (Exodus 20:3–11).

• By failing to do something that God has clearly told us to do in His Word (Matthew 25:31–45).

**Confession**—Telling God about the wrong things we do (sin)

**Repentance**—When we are truly sorry for our sin by feeling regret and sorrow, and we make a change in the behavior that caused us to sin

**Grace**—We don't deserve it and we can't earn it, but grace is what God extends to us when we proclaim Jesus as our Savior and Lord. Grace is possible because Jesus died so that our sins could be forgiven by God. Because of what Jesus did for us at the cross, God shows mercy and kindness to us and forgives us. Someone once said it best: Grace is God's Riches At Christ's Expense.

**Forgiveness**—Because of Jesus' death on the cross, God gives grace to His children by forgiving us when we have confessed and repented of our sins. Then He does an amazing thing! He *forgets* our sin! "For I will forgive their wickedness and will remember their sins no more" (Hebrews 8:12). But God also says that we must forgive others as He forgives us. If we are unwilling to forgive, we can't be forgiven (Matthew 6:14–15). Also, if we are unwilling to forgive, we put up a roadblock between our prayers and God (Mark 11:25).

## ▦ MATERIALS NEEDED:

(Check the Side Trips for additional daily materials)

➲ Bibles

➲ Paper

➲ Pens, pencils, markers

## ▥ MEMORY VERSE:

*Romans 6:14*

## STEP ONE ▢ Practice your memory verse

➲ *Describing sin*

**Ask:** What is sin?
**Say:** Think about something you have done this week that you are really sorry about—something that made God sad.

Maybe it was to say something unkind to someone. Maybe you were disrespectful to your mom or dad. Or maybe you just had mean thoughts about someone else.

**Ask:** What does the Bible say about sin and why it is bad for us? Let's look at a few Scriptures (take turns looking these up and reading them out loud):

John 8:34–36

1 John 3:4–6

Romans 3:23

1 John 3:7–10

1 Corinthians 15:33–34

Hebrews 10:26–27

**Ask:** After reading these Scriptures, what does God think about sin?

• God hates sin.

**Ask:** What can you do about sin?

• First, make sure that Jesus is your Savior and Lord.

• Pray and tell God what you did. *(Confession)*

• Is your heart sorry? Tell God you are sorry. Ask God to help you to never commit that sin again. *(Repentance)*

• Ask Him to forgive you! *(God's forgiveness)*

• Receive His forgiveness and be sure to forgive others (Matthew 6:12) as He has forgiven you. *(Grace)*

**Pray:** Spend some time praying together about sin—and about God's forgiveness! Don't forget to thank Him for sending Jesus to die on the cross for our sins and for His promise of forgiveness.

**STEP TWO** 📖 Say your memory verse

➲ *Some things that cause us to sin*

**Ask:** What are some things that cause us to sin? What would Jesus do?

1. The devil can tempt us by putting thoughts in our minds. Jesus would ignore or resist those thoughts and start thinking about good and lovely things instead. Jesus would battle the devil with the Word of God!

**Read:** Matthew 4:1–11

2. Lack of self-control—sometimes we do the things we know we shouldn't. Other people (even friends and family sometimes) can try to convince us to do the wrong thing. Jesus would only do those things He saw His Father do.

**Read:** John 5:19

3. Pride—when we do not have humble, obedient hearts, the devil can easily cause us to sin. Jesus has a humble, obedient heart.

**Read:** Proverbs 11:2; 16:18; 29:23; Matthew 11:29; Philippians 2:8

4. Selfishness—when we do things we know aren't right because we want something for ourselves. Jesus would give up what He wanted in order to please God.

**Read:** Philippians 2:3; James 3:16; Luke 22:42

**Discuss:** Talk about the things on the list above that are the most difficult for each family member. How can you help each other to stand firm?

**Pray:** Spend some time praying for one another. Pray that God will help your family to submit (surrender) to God and resist the devil (James 4:7). Ask Him to help your family to avoid the things that tempt you to sin.

## STEP THREE   📖 Say your memory verse

➲ *What to do when we sin*

**Say:** All of us will sin from time to time. The key is not to become discouraged but to make every effort to be like Jesus and to ask Him to help us not to sin. If we do this, we will find that the times we sin will become less and less!

**Ask:** What do we do when we blow it?

1. *Confess.* When you confess, you tell God what you did that made Him sad—and maybe other people too. "If we confess our sins, he is faithful and just and will forgive us our sins and purify us from all unrighteousness" (1 John 1:9).

2. *Repent.* Next, tell Him that you are sorry for what you did. In other words, when you confess, you need to be sorry—not just say you are sorry. A repentant heart is a sorry heart. Also, a repentant heart is a changed heart! When you know that what you have done is wrong, you need to do something to change your behavior. See these Scriptures:

John 8:10–11

2 Corinthians 7:8–11

2 Timothy 2:22–26

Hebrews 6:4–6

2 Peter 3:9

**Ask:** Today, if we tell God (confess) what we did (sin) with a sorry heart (repentance), what will He do? (Wait for answers.)

**Say:** Yes, He is going to do something so awesome! He is going to *forgive* us.

**Read:** 1 John 1:9

**Say:** And then He is going to forget we ever committed that sin. God's wonderful gift of forgiving and forgetting is called *grace.*

## STEP FOUR  📖 Say your memory verse

➲ *Jesus is God's answer to our sin*

**Ask:** How can God save us from our sins? (Wait for responses and then reinforce this answer: Because of what Jesus did for us on the cross.)

**Read:** 1 John 2:1–2, 12; Romans 5:6–8; Acts 13:38

**Say:** The Good News is—Jesus came to save us from our sins! What God does for us by forgiving and forgetting our sins is called *grace!*

**Read:** Romans 5:20–21; 6:14

**Say:** God loved us so much that He sent Jesus to die on a cross for us. He died for our sins so that we don't have to. We *do* need to do our best not to sin. We *do* need to ask God to give us the strength not to sin. We want to do only the things that please God.

**Read:** Matthew 9:1–2

**Ask:** How did Jesus show grace to people?

**Say:** Jesus forgave a man his sins because of the great faith of his friends.

**Read:** Luke 7:36–50

**Say:** Jesus forgave a sinful woman because she showed Him great love in doing an act of repentance.

**Read:** Hebrews 8:12

**Say:** Jesus not only forgives our sins, He *forgets* them when we have confessed them with a repentant heart. This is a remarkable thing! The awesome God who knows everything chooses to forget some things—our sins! So, if God forgets them, we can too! He doesn't want us to live feeling guilty—He wants us to live a life more like Jesus! So whenever we have confessed with a repentant heart, we can know without a doubt that God has heard, forgiven, and forgotten our sins! Only a loving God could do such a wonderful thing! His job is to forget; our job is to remember to do everything we can not to commit that sin again and to ask God to help us daily not to sin!

**Say:** God promises to bless when He forgives!

**Read:** Romans 4:7–8

**Say:** We need to try very hard to do what Jesus would do every day and to say what Jesus would say every day! We need to ask God to help us do this—and He will give us this help.

**Read:** Hebrews 10:15–18

**Ask:** How could you show grace to someone else? (Wait for responses.)

**Say:** Jesus taught us that we should forgive others just as He has forgiven us!

**Read:** Luke 11:4

**Pray:** Pray together, asking God to help you forgive others!

**STEP FIVE**  📖 Say your memory verse

➲ *Learning more about confession and God's love for us*

**Let's review:** If we have told God (confession) the wrong thing we did (sin) with a sorry (repentant) heart and we are determined to change how we act so that we do not commit that sin again, He is going to forgive us and forget our sin (forgiveness and grace).

**Ask:** Why does God do that?

• Because He loves us (read John 3:16).

**Ask:** Do we deserve it?

• No, we deserve death (read Romans 6:22–23).

**Say:** Here are two important things God wants us to do when we confess our sins.

**Read:** James 5:16

• One thing God wants us to do is to confess our sins to one another. Confessing our sins within our family, where there is love and trust, allows us to do this.

• After confessing, He wants us to pray for each other so that we won't commit those sins again.

**Pray:** Each person should confess to God at least one thing he wants His forgiveness for. Pray for one another too. (Don't push if someone is reluctant to share—this is a hard thing to do.)

**Say:** We might slip up every now and then, but if we truly want to do the right thing, we will start to sin less and less. We need to ask Jesus to help us not to sin, because we need His help. We can't keep from sinning all by ourselves.

**Read:** 1 Peter 5:8

**Say:** Always remember—our family has an Enemy who would like to cause us to sin. Before we are tempted to do or say a wrong thing, we need to remember to ask ourselves, "What would Jesus do? What would Jesus say?"

**Other helpful Scriptures:** Ephesians 4:25–28; Psalm 4:4

**Say:** We need to know that there are consequences to our sins—we might be punished or someone else might be hurt or damaged. For example, remember King David? A lot of really bad things happened because of his sin!

**Say:** There are two important things we need to do as individuals and as a family:

1. We need to forgive others as we have been forgiven.

**Read:** Matthew 6:14–15; Luke 11:4; Colossians 3:13

2. We need to "leave our life of sin."

**Read:** John 8:1–11; Psalm 4:4; Ephesians 4:25–28

The best way to guard against sin is to do what Psalm 119:11 says: "I have hidden your word in my heart that I might not sin against you."

**Pray:** "Lord, help our family to do only what we see You doing or saying. Forgive us when we fall short and help us to remember that when we confess our sins and are truly sorry, You are waiting to forgive us and forget. Help us to forgive others the way You forgive us. Most of all, help us to hide Your Word in our hearts so that we won't sin against You. Thank You for Your wonderful grace! In Jesus' name we pray. Amen."

## Side Trips

➲ *God's jewels*

## MATERIALS NEEDED:

➲ A box of cornstarch

➲ Several colorful craft jewels (heavy enough to sink) or marbles

## 🕐 PREPARATION:

A parent or older sibling should be familiar with this activity and lead the rest of the family. Mix cornstarch and water to make "clean" mud. Be careful—too much water will dilute the "mud" and too little water will make "cement." You will need to experiment a bit. In order that everyone can see, a large Tupperware or Rubbermaid bowl or container is best. It's probably good to do this on the kitchen counter near the sink so that water can be used to clean up. Put craft jewels or marbles into the mud and be sure they sink to the bottom. Don't let anyone else see you make this mixture, so the jewels are kept a secret.

**Leader:** While you are moving your hand around in the mud and dripping it back into the container, say something like, "Sin is like this mud. Sin damages us and causes our hearts to become dirty too. Sin can also damage other people. But most of all, God hates sin, and when we sin, it makes Him sad.

"But when we realize that we have sinned and we are truly sorry, we can come to God in prayer. We can confess our sin to Him and tell Him how sorry we are. And when we do (the leader should now grab a jewel from the bottom of the container and bring it to the surface), God is already waiting to forgive us and wash away all of the mud to make us clean and shiny like this jewel. (While you are saying this, take a pitcher of water and rinse your hand, while holding on to the jewel.)

"When God forgives us, it's just like becoming a new, sparkling jewel."

**Read** James 5:16
**Say:** Each of us needs to think of one thing we have done in the last week or two that made God sad. If it was something that involved another family member, we need to try very hard

to go to that person and confess what we have done or said. Then we need to ask for forgiveness from that person and from God. Confessing sin and asking for forgiveness is very hard to do. We need to ask God to help us! (Give an example of something you may have done and go to the person you need to confess to. For example, " John, I am very sorry that I got angry with you Saturday night. I was tired and shouldn't have taken it out on you. Will you forgive me?" After "John" has given his forgiveness, read Mark 11:25 out loud.)

**Activity:** Encourage everyone to take a few minutes to go to at least one other family member to ask for forgiveness and/or to forgive. If this is still difficult, suggest that they write a note asking for forgiveness or extending forgiveness.

Afterwards, instruct each person to "dig" for a jewel in the "clean" mud. Remind them as they dig around in the "mud" that it represents our sin.

Tell them as they pull a jewel out of the mud that God has now forgiven them. As you rinse off their hand and the jewel, say something like, "Now that you have confessed your sin and because you are sorry for it, you can be forgiven and washed clean of that sin—so that God can make your life a beautiful jewel." Encourage each person to keep that jewel in a place where it will always remind him or her of God's grace and forgiveness.

⊃ *Prayer pennies*

 MATERIALS NEEDED:

⊃ A large jar of pennies

At the beginning of this journey, give every family member one hundred pennies in a Ziplock bag. Tell each person to keep the pennies in a place where they can easily find them. Put a bowl onto a counter or the dining-room table. Tell each family member to put in a penny if they do or say anything that doesn't please God. Instruct them to pray when they put their penny or pennies into the bowl, asking God to forgive them. This can be done anonymously.

At the end of each day or once a week, have a prayer time together. Share your hearts, confess and repent, and ask for forgiveness from others or forgive those who need to be forgiven (even if it is someone not in your family). Be sure to praise God and rejoice in His forgiveness once each sin has been confessed.

Shine up the pennies with brass cleaner or baking soda and water as a symbol of God's forgiveness and a visible reminder of how He cleans us up. Start over again for another week or however long you have decided. At an agreed upon time, count the pennies and, with thanksgiving to God for His grace, spend the money on something special for your family such as pizza or ice cream.

➲ *Up in smoke!*

▤ MATERIALS NEEDED:

---

➲ A deep metal bowl lined with heavy-duty foil

➲ Matches or a lighter

➲ Paper

➲ Pens or markers

**Ask:** What are some sins that can keep God from hearing and answering our prayers?

• Talk about the sin of unforgiveness and how it can keep us from having our prayers answered (read Mark 11:25).

• Talk about the sin of anger (read 1 Timothy 2:8).

• Talk about the sin of not taking care of people who have needs (read Proverbs 21:13).

• Talk about the sin of praying to be seen by men (read Matthew 6:5).

**Write** down (or draw pictures) of anything you have done that may be keeping God from answering your prayers. If you can't think of anything, ask the Lord to show you an area in your life that is not pleasing to Him.

Put the papers in a deep foil-lined bowl and spend some time praying for forgiveness. Have a parent light the papers on fire and watch all of your sins go up in smoke—a symbol of God's forgiveness—as one person reads Psalm 32:1–2.

➲ *People just like us*

**Read** these stories of people in the Bible who sinned and were forgiven:

• King David (2 Samuel 11:1–12:13)

• The Prodigal Son (Luke 15:11–24)

• The woman who washed Jesus' feet (Luke 7:36–50)

• The paralytic (Luke 5:22–26)

**Ask:** Which story do you like the best? Why? How do these stories make you feel?

## HOW TO MAKE THIS
## A JOURNEY FOR A LIFETIME

1. Practice forgiving others! Show them the same grace that God has shown you.

2. Do your best to watch for danger signs, as the Enemy will try to get you to sin. Be determined to have victory!

3. Write down your testimony. What has God done in your life? How did you come to know Him? How has He forgiven you?

4. Practice your testimony so that you feel comfortable telling it to others.

5. Read 1 Peter 3:15. Always be prepared to share your testimony.

6. Keep short accounts with God each day of your life!

# Prayers of Thanksgiving and Praise

*That my heart may sing to you and not be silent.*
*O LORD my God, I will give you thanks forever.*

PSALM 30:12

One day, when I was in a particular hurry, I couldn't find my car keys. The more I looked, the more exasperated I got! My youngest son, David, watched me for a while and finally said, "Mom—why don't you pray?" Duh! Why didn't I think of that? So, he and I prayed together that the Lord would show me where my keys were . . . and we found them almost immediately afterwards, because I "suddenly remembered" where they were. Coincidence? No—God incidence! We gave the Lord thanks for helping me to find my keys, and I have never forgotten the lesson my son taught me about giving the Lord an opportunity to help me so that He could get the honor and praise through our prayers of thanksgiving! What has the Lord done in your life lately—big or small? Have you thanked Him?

Every day God gives me lots of opportunities to give Him praise—even on days when things aren't going so well. I find that if I will praise God even when I don't feel like it or when things aren't going quite the way I want them to, my heart can be lifted high above anything that is trying to overwhelm or discourage me.

Did you know that praising God is prayer? When you focus your praise on God, you are communicating (talking) with Him. What is prayer? Talking with God. One day, each of us will join in the heavenly chorus of praise before the throne of our awesome Lord. So this journey will give your family a wonderful opportunity to learn to experience what we will one day spend our days doing in heaven!

## WHAT YOUR FAMILY WILL DISCOVER ON THIS JOURNEY

⋋ *Good reasons to give thanks*

⋋ *Creative ways to thank the Lord for little things and big things*

⋋ *How to live a lifestyle of thanksgiving*

⋋ *What it means to praise God*

⋋ *How to express praise as prayer*

⋋ *Some fun ways to praise the Lord*

⋋ *How to live your lives in such a way that the Lord is continually praised*

## 🕐 PREPARATION:

You may wish to write down the Scriptures for each day and be ready to assign them to various members of the family. Then you won't have to wait while everyone looks up verses.

## 📋 MATERIALS NEEDED:

➲ Check out "Praise Puppets" under the Side Trips section of this journey before you begin.

## 📖 MEMORY VERSES:

*Isaiah 12:4; Psalm 104:33; Psalm 150:6 (You can split these up among different family members or be challenged to memorize them all!)*

**STEP ONE** 📖 Practice your memory verse

➲ *Reasons to thank God*

## 📋 MATERIALS NEEDED:

➲ Dry-erase board or chalkboard

**Ask:** What are some reasons you can think of to thank God? (Give everyone a chance to answer. Use a dry-erase board or chalkboard to write down responses—this would be a good task to give a child.)

**Do:** Have each member of the family who can read look up one to three of the Scriptures listed below under Reasons to Give Thanks. Compare the answers you gave with these. How were your answers similar or different?

### REASONS TO GIVE THANKS

- Because Jesus gave thanks (Matthew 14:19; 26:27–28)

- Because it is God's will for us in Christ Jesus (1 Thessalonians 5:16–18)

- Because He is good and His love endures forever (1 Chronicles 16:34)

- Because of His righteousness (Psalm 7:17)

• Because His name is near (Psalm 75:1)

• Because His faithfulness continues through all generations (Psalm 100:4–5)

• Because of His unfailing love and His wonderful deeds for men (Psalm 107:21)

• Because He answers prayer and saves us (Psalm 118:21)

• Because He meets our needs and makes us rich in every way so that we can be generous to others (2 Corinthians 9:10–11)

**Do:** Go around in a circle and finish this sentence: "Lord, I thank You because _____."
**Add:** Make this a prayer of thanks!

## STEP TWO 📖 Say your memory verses

➲ *Showing thanks*

**Ask:** How do you show God that you are a thankful person? (Give everyone a chance to respond.)
**Ask:** How did people in the Bible express thanks to God? (Have different family members look up and read these passages.)

• By being generous to others (2 Corinthians 9:10–11)

• By calling on His name and making known to the nations what He has done (1 Chronicles 16:8)

• By singing praises to His name (Psalm 7:17)

• By giving Him glory (Psalm 69:30)

- By sacrificing thank offerings to the Lord (Psalm 107:19–22) (See below.)

- By prayer (Philippians 4:6)

**Pray:** Give thanks to the Lord in prayer right now!

## STEP THREE   📖 Say your memory verses
➲ *A thank offering*

In the Old Testament, a thank offering was made to the Lord as an act of thanksgiving for blessings received from Him. It was part of formal worship.

Today, in a similar way, as a family, sacrifice a thank offering to the Lord for the blessings He has given you. There is no wrong or right way to do this, so you can make your thank offering something unique. Maybe you could actively express one or more of the things suggested in Journey Two as a family thank offering. Could you tell someone about Jesus? Could you be generous to someone in need? Could you sing praises to His name? Plan a special way to express your thanks to Him today. You can even do something creative: Make a poster or a collage of thanks, take pictures of things you are thankful for, make a special thank offering album—you can add to this on a continual basis. Decide together what you will do and offer it to the Lord with thanksgiving.

## STEP FOUR   📖 Say your memory verses
➲ *Things we are not thankful for*

**Say:** Think of at least one thing you are not thankful for. Remember, sometimes the Lord allows circumstances into our lives that help us to grow and mature as Christians. These things are not always pleasant or easy.

**Read:** Take turns reading the following Scriptures out loud:

- Philippians 4:4–7

- Colossians 3:15–17

- Ephesians 5:19–20

- 1 Thessalonians 5:16–18

- Hebrews 12:7–11

**Ask:** Did your feelings change about the things you are not thankful for after reading these Scriptures? Why or why not?

**Say:** God does not say we must be thankful *for* all of the things that happen in our lives, but He does say that we should be thankful *in the midst* of them.

**Ask:** In these difficult circumstances, whether it involves you or not, how is it possible for Christians to give thanks?

**Discuss** how joy, singing, peace, and prayer relate to thanking God in the midst of circumstances where you do not feel thankful at first.

**Pray** together about whatever you are not thankful for, asking the Lord to allow your hearts to be thankful in the midst of your circumstances.

**STEP FIVE** 📖 Say your memory verses

➲ *Ways to say thank you to God*

**Read** Psalm 100 out loud today. It is a psalm written just for the purpose of giving thanks to God.

**Make** a list of all the ways the psalmist says to give thanks.

**Activity:** As a family, write your own psalm of thanksgiving to the Lord and speak it out loud to Him! Give it to the Lord as a thank offering for all the ways He has blessed you.

#  Side Trips

⊃ *Balloon thank-you note*

## ▤ MATERIALS NEEDED:

⊃ A Mylar balloon that says "Thank You"

⊃ Lightweight paper

⊃ Hole punch

⊃ Ribbon

⊃ Markers or colored pencils

Cut the paper into squares big enough to write a message on. Have each family member carefully write or draw something they are thankful for on his or her piece of paper. You can do more than one if you wish. Begin with something similar to "Lord, thank You for . . ." or "Thank You, Jesus, for . . ." Punch a hole at the top of each piece of paper and attach the papers to your balloon with ribbon. Make sure that the weight of your papers will still allow your balloon to fly. If you want, include a square with your family's name and phone number and your e-mail or street address and ask whoever finds the balloon to let you know. It might give you an opportunity to share Christ with someone!

⊃ *Celebration supper*

Have a special celebration from time to time to honor God for His goodness to you. Prepare a special meal and invite friends or neighbors who don't know Jesus as Savior and Lord. Explain that you want to share what He has done in your lives with others and tell them why you are thankful.

### ➲ Good deed box

Have a special box or basket where "good deeds" can be shared. If someone in your family did a nice thing, put his or her name in the box with a short description about what he or she did. Once a week during a meal or other special time, pull out each name one at a time. The person who put the name in the box should tell why they are thankful for that family member. After each story, the whole family can say something like, "Give thanks to the Lord, for He is good." Remember to steer the conversation back to what God does in and through us so that pride will not become a factor. Remember—it's not what we do but what God does in and through us!

### ➲ Thank-You book

As a family, make a large book out of construction paper and yarn, or some other creative way. Decorate the front. Whenever a family member is thankful for something or someone, he or she can write it (or draw it, for younger children) in the book. Put the book in a place where everyone will see it often and be reminded to write down what they are thankful for. Watch and see what a thankful family you become as you look through your book to remember the Lord's blessings.

### ➲ Thank-You letter

Once a month, or whenever it seems good to you, write a letter to God thanking Him for all that He has done to bless your family, what He has done in the lives of others, how He has worked in different situations, for answering prayers, and so on. You can use your thank-you book or just what comes to mind as you write this letter together. Decide as a family what you will do with these letters. You may want to put them into your Thank-You Book from time to time.

### ➲ Thank offerings

Whenever God has done something your family wishes to thank Him for, give Him a special thank offering. One good way is to do something special for another family. It would be a good way to share the blessings of Christ with your neighbors or with other families that don't know Jesus. For example, you might welcome a new baby at your house or Dad just got a new job. Celebrate what the Lord has done in your lives by inviting others over for an evening of board games or a video with ice-cream sundaes. Be creative. Just be sure to let the invited family know why you are celebrating and that you are giving thanks to God.

## STEP SIX ⬚ Practice your memory verses
### ➲ Praising God

### ▤ MATERIALS NEEDED:

➲ Dry-erase board or chalkboard or paper and pencils

**Say:** What does it mean to praise God? Praise is a joyful expression of our hearts and a way to honor the Lord of the universe. In Hebrew, praise means giving glory to God. In the Greek, it means to give praise to what is worthy of praise. The emphasis in Scripture is man giving praise to God. Praise in the Bible is most often expressed in poetry and/or in song. The angels praise God continuously, and all of creation praises God.

Have someone in your family read Revelation 5:13. Jesus praised the Father, so we should too!

**Read:** Luke 10:17–21

**Make** a list of all of the reasons we should give praise to God. Now spend some time giving praise to Him. You can use "Lord, we praise You because _____," or "Lord, we praise You for _____." Try to keep your focus on *praise* rather than thanksgiving. Giving thanks is different from singing praise. Here is the difference: Thanking God is honoring Him because of something He *does*. Praising God is honoring Him because of who He *is!*

**Read** some or all of the following: Exodus 15:2; Deuteronomy 32:3; 2 Samuel 22:47, 50; 1 Chronicles 16:25; 29:10; 2 Chronicles 5:13; Ezra 3:10–13; Psalms 7:17; 9:1–2; 103:1–2; 146:2; Luke 1:68 (Zechariah was John the Baptist's father); 1 Peter 1:3

# Side Trip

➲ *Baskets of praise and thanksgiving*

Get two small boxes or baskets to place on the table where you eat meals. Label one "Praises." Label the other "Thanksgiving." Put some small pieces of paper, a notepad, or 3 x 5 cards next to them. At least once a day for a week or more, have each family member put something in each basket. Put in as many things as you want! In the "Praises" basket, write: "Jesus, I praise You because You are . . ." In the "Thanksgiving" basket, write "Jesus, thank You for . . ." You can put your name on the cards or not—that's up to you. At one meal a day, whichever is the best attended by everyone in the family, take turns reading through the cards and then pray.

**STEP SEVEN**  📖 Say your memory verses

➔ *A–Z praises*

**Read:** Psalm 66:4

**Ask:** Can you remember some of the praises you lifted up to God last time?

Take turns, beginning with the letter A through the letter Z, saying, "Lord, You are _____ (put in a word of praise)." For example: "Lord, You are *awesome!*" Try to memorize each one as you go around. See if you can remember all twenty-six praise words at the end! If you need help, see the list in Journey #11, "Prayer Parties."

**STEP EIGHT**  📖 Say your memory verses

➔ *Writing a song or psalm of praise to the Lord as a family*

**Read** Psalms 8, 67, 84, 92, 100, 103, 145, 148, 150 to get ideas! Maybe each member of the family who reads can choose one of these psalms to read to the others. Pair up prereaders with older siblings or parents. Write your own psalm of praise. When you are finished, offer your song or psalm of praise to the Lord. If you play instruments, you may wish to include them as you praise God. Or you could use a tambourine or other music makers to enhance your expression of praise to the Lord. If you are all too shy, just take turns reading or read together your praise to God. Make it a prayer to Him.

# 🌲 Side Trips

➲ *Living Stones*

## 📋 MATERIALS NEEDED:

➲ At least one stone per person (the stones should be as flat as possible and large enough to write on)

➲ Permanent markers

**Read and discuss** Luke 19:28–40

**Activity.** Clean the stones thoroughly. Using permanent markers (wide, medium, or fine tip depending upon the size of your rock), write a Scripture verse that gives praise to God. Each rock should have a different Scripture. You can do several things with your stones:

• Place them in your garden or along your walkway—or where you will see them as you go in and out of your home. Remember to praise the Lord when you see them.

• Place one stone in each room of the house (as a doorstopper or paperweight). Whenever you go in or out of a room, say the praise Scripture written on the rock.

• Give them to family, neighbors, or friends. You might want to decorate them a bit more and tie a ribbon around them if you give them away. You could also keep one set at home and have a set to give away. Think of all the people who will be praising the Lord each day because they saw a stone that reminded them to do so—a living stone!

• Can you think of other ways to use your living praise stones?

**Read:** Isaiah 38:19 to dedicate your living stones as an offering of praise to the Lord!

**Dad or Mom:** Tell a story about God's faithfulness to you at some point in your life.

**Read:** 1 Peter 2:4–5 and discuss how you can be like "a living stone."

**Pray** that God will build your family into a spiritual house filled with living stones.

### ➲ *Praise puppets*

Get one or more puppets, if you already have them at home. If not, make them out of paper bags or socks. Take turns having the puppets praise God! This is especially good for shy family members. You may wish to have these ready to go and use them before you begin this journey! They might come in handy each day.

⁂

## HOW TO MAKE THIS
## A JOURNEY FOR A LIFETIME

1. "If anyone speaks, he should do it as one speaking the very words of God. If anyone serves, he should do it with the strength God provides, so that in all things God may be praised through Jesus Christ. To him be the glory and the power for ever and ever. Amen" (1 Peter 4:11). Make praising God daily and continually a natural part of your everyday life!

2. *Every Little Thing.* Make thanking God a lifestyle. Learn to give thanks for everything—even the smallest things that happen. For example, if you lose something and then find it—thank the Lord. If you have two tests on

the same day and one gets canceled—thank the Lord.
If you get to have spaghetti for dinner and you really
like spaghetti—thank the Lord. These are little things,
but God cares about every little thing in your life. Give
Him thanks in *all* things! Once you learn to be thankful
for the small things, you will certainly have no problem
thanking the Lord in the big things! Becoming a thankful person will help you to develop a strong, healthy relationship with the Lord in prayer and praise!

# The Anytime and Anywhere of Prayer

*After he had dismissed them,
he went up on a mountainside
by himself to pray.*

MATTHEW 14:23

When I first met my husband, Dave, I wanted to spend time with him. I wanted to know everything about him. In short, I wanted to be with him as much as possible because he had captured my heart. This is how our relationship to the Lord should be—and so much more! He is to be our first love, the one we seek above all others—even above our family relationships. We should long to spend time with Him and to know everything about Him.

How do we get to know the Lord in the deepest, most intimate way possible? We set apart special times to be with Him . . . just Him! This is called a "quiet time." These quiet times can be anywhere . . . but the most private, special place to meet with God will be your "prayer closet." Remember, your communication with the Lord is always ongoing. You can meet with Him anywhere at anytime; however, the time and place you set apart for an intentional meeting with Him will always be the most precious and powerful of your day!

When I consider the various prayer closets I've been in over the years and the many ways I have met the Lord in quiet and through journaling, there is no physical place that stands out in my memory. There is, however, a treasure within me that has been growing and building—the treasure of knowing Jesus more each day. As a family, we talk a lot about daily walking with Jesus, becoming more like Him day by day and doing and saying only those things He would do and say. These things cannot happen unless we spend time with Him in daily prayer, study, and worship—and unless we are continually aware of the presence of Christ within us: "Christ in you, the hope of glory" (Colossians 1:27b).

The time you set aside each day to meet with God is the best investment you will make in your day. This is where the learning and growth occur in us! I encourage you to practice His presence individually and as a family—daily.

## WHAT YOUR FAMILY WILL DISCOVER ON THIS JOURNEY

➤ *The Bible has much to say about different ways of praying*

➤ *How different people in the Bible prayed*

➤ *People pray differently in different circumstances*

➤ *You can pray anytime, anywhere, and any way you feel led by the Holy Spirit*

➤ *You can pray about* anything—*big or small*

➤ *It is important to pray by yourself in your prayer closet and to pray with your family and others*

➤ *It is important to set aside some time each day to meet with God*

 MEMORY VERSE:

*Matthew 6:6*

**STEP ONE** 📖 Practice your memory verse

➲ *We can pray anywhere*

**Read:** Psalm 139:8

**Say:** The Lord can hear our prayers no matter where we are. Jonah discovered that the Lord could hear his prayer from the belly of a whale. Even in the highest heights or the deepest depths, the Lord is with us. Talking with God in certain places can have a positive effect on our prayers. Locations that we consider holy, like a church or a quiet place, can increase our feeling of reverence for God. They can help us to feel closer to Him. But we can experience this reverence (respect) in our own prayer closets, wherever we might be (a bedroom, a kitchen table, a chair in a quiet corner).

**Read:** Matthew 6:5–6 (part of this is your memory verse)

**Ask:** Where are some places you like to pray? (Have family members share.)

**Ask:** Why do you like to pray there? Does it make you feel different when you pray in different places? Why or why not?

**Ask:** Do you have a "prayer closet"—a special private place where you can get to know God and spend special times with Him? A special time with God is a quiet time.

**Say:** If you don't already have a place, think about somewhere that you can get alone with God—your own prayer closet. You might want to have a basket or container with your Bible, your journal, and pens that you leave in that place. You can have other special places too—but this will be your main meeting place with God. It will be the place where you come to spend time alone with Him (your quiet time). It will need to be quiet and away from distractions—other people or noises.

Even though there might be a special place where you meet with God, always remember that we can pray anywhere—in the car, on the playground, at work—anywhere! Praying what is on our hearts is more important than where we pray.

**Activity:** Help each family member to find a "prayer closet" somewhere in your home. It can be indoors or outdoors, depending on where you live and what your climate is like. As a family, "set apart" each person's prayer closet by praying that he or she will meet God there in a special way each day. Make an agreement that you will all respect the space around one another's prayer closets whenever they are in use.

## STEP TWO  📖 Say your memory verse

➲ *We can pray anytime*

**Say:** We can pray anytime! In fact, God wants us to pray all the time. Have different members of the family look up the following Scriptures to read:

- 1 Thessalonians 5:17

- Ephesians 6:18

- 2 Timothy 1:3

Now we know that we can and should talk to God anytime. But we need to find some time to focus just on Him. Each of us should find a time each day to set aside for talking with God in the special place chosen to be our "prayer closet."

Look up these Scriptures about different times to pray:

*Morning*—Psalm 88:13; Mark 1:35

*Night*—Psalm 63:6; Luke 6:12–16

*Day and night*—1 Thessalonians 3:10; 1 Timothy 5:5

**Ask:** When is the best time for you to pray? (Wait for responses.) Remember—we can pray anytime! However, we need to choose a time during the day to spend a longer time with God in prayer. We can also ask Him to help us walk with Him all day long in prayer.

**Activity:** Help each family member select at least one block of time each day to spend alone with God in his or her prayer closet. The amount of time will depend upon age and spiritual maturity. Your youngest children may spend five to ten minutes in their prayer closets, while older youth and parents may spend half an hour, an hour, or longer each day. Help each person to determine what time commitment is best for him or her right now and write it down. This will help you to encourage one another to keep that commitment daily.

**Please Note:** This should not be a legalistic requirement. It will take time to develop a good, solid daily pattern. Keep encouraging your family. Some families choose to have their quiet times at a similar time for a while so that everyone acquires a strong daily habit.

**STEP THREE** 📖 Say your memory verse

➲ *There are many ways to pray to the Lord*

**Say:** We have learned that we can pray anytime and anywhere. Today we're going to talk about some different ways people can pray.

**Ask:** What do you do with your body when you pray? (Take turns sharing.) Do you pray the same way every time?

**Say:** Most people pray the way they were taught. Usually, the head is bowed, the eyes are closed, and the hands are folded. Is that what you do? There is nothing wrong with praying this way! God is honored because of what we say and because of what is in our hearts. What we do with our bodies should just be an expression of what is in our hearts. We should never try to "impress" God or other people when we pray—even other members of our own family. Our prayers are always to be directed to God, not to the people around us. Remember the story of the hypocrites, who prayed on the street corners to be seen by everyone (Matthew 6:5)?

We are going to spend some time on this journey learning how different people in the Bible prayed. Maybe you will want to try something new as you pray. Sometimes the position of prayer depends upon the feeling in your heart and in your spirit. If you wish to humble yourself before the Lord, you may want to kneel or lie flat on the floor. If you wish to confess sin or to express your repentance, you may want to bow your head. If you are expressing deep need or great joy—you may wish to stand and raise your hands! Do you see? God is not concerned with your position as much as He is in the condition of your heart. What we do with our bodies when we pray is a way to express how we feel about our spiritual condition and how we feel about God.

• We may pray quietly, as Hannah did (1 Samuel 1:9–18).

• We may shout our praise to the Lord, as David did (Psalms 66:1–4; 71:23; 95:1; 98:4–6).

**Pray:** Spend some time praying quietly.

**Pray:** Take turns shouting out praise to God. Don't force anyone who is not comfortable but be encouraging. One way to help the shy ones is to take turns saying, "Lord, You are _____!" (Fill in the blanks!)

**Pray:** Spend some time together praying that the Lord will teach you many new things about prayer each day of your journey. Ask Him to touch your hearts and help you to learn how to pray in whatever ways the Holy Spirit may direct.

## STEP FOUR 📖 Say your memory verse

➲ *We can pray bowing our heads or our bodies*

**Say:** Bowing our heads is usually the first thing any of us learns about prayer. It is one way to focus, to show reverence (respect), and to be submissive (obedient) to God. It is probably one way to pray that we have all done before.

**Read** these Scriptures together (you might wish to talk about the events preceding the passages): Genesis 24:26–27; Exodus 34:8–9

**Pray:** Have each family member give one or two prayer requests. Bow your heads or bow to the ground and pray over those requests together.

## STEP FIVE 📖 Say your memory verse

➲ *We can pray kneeling*

**Say:** Kneeling has always been a universal sign of submission (obedience).

**Read** these Scriptures together: Daniel 6:10; Luke 22:39– 44; Matthew 15:25; 2 Chronicles 6:12–14. Note that in the 2 Chronicles passage, Solomon not only knelt down but also spread out his hands toward heaven (see Step Six). This indicates that his head was not bowed but that he was looking up. When King Solomon knelt down to pray during the dedication of the temple, he was admitting publicly that he was God's servant (remember that kneeling is a sign of submission or obedience to God). Reaching out his hands—a gesture not unlike a beggar might make—indicated he was asking something from God. King Solomon prayed this way because of the condition of his heart. He did what he felt led to do out of recognizing the greatness of God—the King above all kings.

Sometimes, we might start out praying in one position and feel led by the Lord to change. For example, we might begin our prayer by bowing our heads, and as the Lord shows us the sin in our lives, we might get down on our knees or lie prostrate (facedown) on the floor before Him. Sometimes we might begin our prayer time with worship, and the realization of the awesome God we serve might bring us to our feet with our hands raised as we offer praise to Him.

**Pray:** Today, pray for your unsaved family and friends, as you kneel together before the Lord. If you feel led to, spread out your hands toward heaven, as King Solomon did. Try turning your face toward heaven as well.

**Discuss** how the change of position made you feel. Was it a good way to talk with God? Did it help you to focus on the Lord? Why or why not? (Each person's experience may be different.)

## STEP SIX  📖 Say your memory verse

⊃ *We can pray with our hands raised, with holy hands lifted up, or with our hands spread out*

**Say:** From ancient times, upraised hands have been a sign of both praise and petition (asking). The Hebrews used their hands to show their dependence upon God and their respect for Him. Lifting up holy hands was the common prayer posture among the Jews and the early Christians. Lifting their hands symbolized an expectant attitude and trust in God—that He would fill their empty hands with His blessings.

**Interesting Note:** One of the Hebrew words for praise (*yadah*), derived from the Hebrew word for hand (*yad*), means "to stretch out the hand."

**Read** the following Scriptures together: Exodus 9:29; 17:10–13; 1 Kings 8:54–55; Psalms 63:4; 141:2; 1 Timothy 2:8

**Pray:** Today, pray for the leaders of your nation, your state, and your community. Lift up holy hands together as you do. Pray that God will give them wisdom and discernment. Pray for their health and protection. Pray for their families.

## STEP SEVEN   📖 Say your memory verse

➲ *We can pray standing*

**Say:** Standing is a sign of reverence and respect. We stand for our national anthem when it is played. We stand up when people in authority come into the room. Standing should also be a sign of reverence and respect before the Lord when we come into His presence.

**Read:** Stand together and read these Scriptures: 1 Chronicles 23:28–31; 2 Chronicles 20:2–9; Luke 18:9–14. After each Scripture, discuss what happened. What is God teaching you about standing to pray? What made the biggest impression on you?

**Praise:** Stand together and give praise to God. Take turns thanking Him for all of the blessings He has brought into your lives. If you want, say short sentence prayers like this: "Lord, I praise You for _____."

## STEP EIGHT   📖 Say your memory verse

➲ *We can pray prostrate (lying facedown) before the Lord*

**Say:** In the Bible this position appears to be taken in times of deep, intense, emotional prayer. There is no more humble position than this one, as demonstrated by Jesus, David, and Moses, who all came before the Lord on their faces.

**Read:** Deuteronomy 9:18–20, 25–27; 1 Chronicles 21:16–17; Matthew 26:39

**Ask:** Why did each of these men fall on their faces before the Lord? Were their reasons different?

**Pray:** Today, think of some deeply important needs—your own or someone else's. Perhaps someone is struggling with a life-threatening disease or some kind of life crisis. Perhaps sin has been weighing you down—this would be an appropriate position in which to confess and ask the Lord for forgiveness. Or maybe you need to ask God something very important. Come before the Lord together on behalf of these requests, lying facedown before the Lord. You can pray quietly by yourself or pray out loud with others.

**Ask:** How did lying on your face before the Lord make you feel? Was it hard to humble yourself before the Lord this way? Maybe it was hard to do with your family. When you have the opportunity, try this posture of prayer when you are by yourself.

**Pray:** Spend some time in prayer together thanking Him for what He is teaching you about prayer.

**STEP NINE**   📖 Say your memory verse

➲ *We can pray looking up*

**Read** this passage of Scripture together: Mark 6:39–44

**Discuss** how you would have felt as a family if you had been there that day and experienced such a remarkable event.

**Pray:** As you give thanks for your meals today, look up to heaven as you do. Spend some time together as a family thanking the Lord for the way He has provided everything you need—your food, your clothing, your housing. Look toward heaven when you pray.

**STEP TEN** 📖 Say your memory verse

➲ *Watch and pray*

**Read** Mark 14:38 and Luke 21:36. The Scriptures tell us to "watch and pray." Discuss what it means to do this. Why is it important? How are you tempted by the Enemy? How would things be different if you were alert enough to always watch and pray? How can you help one another to watch and pray?

**Pray** through your local newspaper. Pray about world, national, and local news. Ask the Lord to show you what He wants to do about these things and how He wants you to be involved, as His praying people. He wants you to watch what is going on around you—and then pray!

**Discuss** how you can help your neighbors in times of crisis or fear.

## ⛄ *Side Trips*

➲ *Corporate prayer*

**Ask:** Did you know that praying together with others is called corporate (group) prayer?

**Say:** It is important to pray alone in our prayer closets and to pray with one or more prayer partners. When our family prays together, we are prayer partners.

**Read:** Matthew 18:20

**Say:** It is also very important for Christians to join with other Christians in groups or as a church family to pray.

**Read** what the early Christians in the book of Acts did when they got together: Acts 1:12–14; 4:23–25, 31; 12:5, 12; 13:3; 20:36

**Discussion:** Do you see a pattern? What did the early church do when they got together? Discuss how to find opportunities to gather with others to pray. Maybe you can invite another family to your home to pray together. Or your family can attend a prayer gathering at your church. If you have never prayed with other brothers and sisters in Christ, you will find it a powerful experience and one that pleases the Lord very much. Could you get together with others for an event like the National Day of Prayer or invite neighbors over for a Prayer Party? (See Journey #11.)

### ➲ Laying on of hands

**Say:** The laying on of hands as a way of consecrating (setting someone apart) to a special purpose appears in both the Old Testament and the New Testament.

**Read:** Numbers 27:18–23; Deuteronomy 34:9

**Say:** When Moses consecrated Joshua for service, "he laid his hands on him and commissioned him, as the LORD instructed" (Numbers 27:23). Later, in Deuteronomy 34:9, we are told that "Joshua . . . was filled with the spirit of wisdom because Moses has laid his hands on him." So in the Old Testament the laying on of hands was associated with consecrating for service and filling with power.

**Read:** Matthew 19:13–15; Mark 8:22–25; Luke 4:40; 13:10–13; Acts 9:17–19

**Say:** Jesus and His disciples didn't lay hands on people for "show." They did it because the act of touching—laying on of hands—connected people with God's power and God's blessing. It is always appropriate to lay hands on people and pray. This simple act can release God's power into the lives of people. Remember—this is not a magical formula for getting what we want from God. This is, instead, following the example of Jesus.

There were several special circumstances in which the laying on of hands was recorded in the Bible: for healing, for blessing, for commissioning (setting apart, appointing, ordaining) people for service, and for the receiving of spiritual gifts.

**Read** the following Scriptures together to have an example of each and discuss what you learn:

• *Healing*—Matthew 8:1–3; Luke 6:19. The power of the Holy Spirit flowed from Jesus' touch. Jesus and His disciples healed many people through the simple act of touch—connecting those in need of healing with the Healer. Can you find some other examples in the Bible where people were healed through prayer and the laying on of hands? Hint: Try Acts 28:7–9.

• *Blessing*—Mark 10:13–16. When people brought little children to Jesus to be blessed, "he took the children in his arms, put his hands on them and blessed them." (See Journey #12, "The Family Blessing.")

• *Setting apart for service*—Acts 6:1–6; 13:1–3. In Acts, church leaders and missionaries are set apart (ordained, commissioned) by the laying on of hands. This practice continues today in ordination services for pastors and commissioning services for missionaries and other church leaders.

• *Receiving spiritual gifts through the power of the Holy Spirit*—Acts 8:17; 1 Timothy 4:14; 2 Timothy 1:6–7. In Acts, people received the Holy Spirit through the laying on of hands, and the epistles to Timothy show that he received pastoral, teaching, and preaching gifts in the same way.

**Ask:** Which family member needs extra special prayer today? If that is not clear to you, take turns laying hands on each member of the family and praying for him or her. Pray a special blessing on each one as you do so. (See Journey #12, "The Family Blessing.")

## ➲ *Anointing with oil*

**Say:** In the Bible, applying oil in a sacred service—anointing with oil—occurred for two reasons: (1) when a person or place was to be set apart for God's use, and (2) when praying for healing. Oil represents the Holy Spirit, as you read in 1 Samuel 16:13. Anointing with oil signifies that a person or place has been set apart by the power of the Holy Spirit. When we anoint people to ask for healing, we are asking for the power of the Holy Spirit to touch their lives.

Here are some Scripture passages about anointing with oil as a way of setting apart a person or place for special service.

• Moses anointed the tabernacle with oil (Leviticus 8:10–11).

• Aaron and his sons were ordained (set apart) as priests by God (Leviticus 8:12).

•. David was anointed with oil and set apart as king of Israel (1 Samuel 16:13, Psalms 23:5; 89:20). Other kings—Saul, Jehu, and Solomon for example—were anointed with oil also.

Has your home been dedicated (set apart) to God's use? Whenever we have moved to a new home, we always anoint the doorposts of each door (inside and out) with oil, claiming it for Christ and His purposes. We dedicate it for His use, and pray that He will use our home to bring many people to Himself. We pray that it will be a place of hospitality and warmth, a place where every person who enters will feel loved and cared for—and where they will sense the presence of God. You never really know what may have gone on in your home before it was yours. So, this is also a good way to serve notice to the Enemy that he cannot hang around.

How about dedicating (setting apart) an office, or a classroom, or any other place where one or more members of your family have influence?

If you build a new home or add on, write Scriptures on the unpainted walls (in pencil) and anoint the home with oil, dedicating it to the Lord. (Please heed the warning about using a pencil—pen and markers can bleed through a freshly painted wall. We learned this through a painful personal experience!)

Are you wondering what kind of oil to use? That is probably not important to the Lord as long as you pray that He will use it for His purposes and as long as you use it in a way that honors Him. Our family uses olive oil, and we have a special container for it. (The Bible also talks about an anointing oil with spices in it, while olive oil is most often referred to for using with lamps.) We prayed that God would set our oil apart for His use. Isn't it interesting that we can pray to ask the Lord to set apart something that will then be used to set apart people and places or to use in prayer for healing?

Missionaries (short or long term), pastors, elders, church leaders—anyone who is being set apart for ministry in the church—should be anointed with oil and prayed for earnestly.

Here are some Scripture passages about anointing with oil for the purpose of healing.

• Jesus sent the disciples out two by two. Read Mark 6:12–13 to learn about one of the things that happened.

• Read James 5:13–14 to see what Christians are called to do when there is a need for healing.

When someone is sick, lay hands upon him and anoint him with oil. Remember—Jesus' disciples were able to heal the sick. Jesus has called us to be His disciples today. Therefore, He has given us the ability to heal in the powerful name of Jesus Christ. If the person is seriously ill, remember that Scripture tells us to call for the elders (James 5:14). There is much power in obedience.

**Note:** Remember, sometimes God chooses to answer our prayers in a different way than we expect Him to. This is where faith comes in. Faith is trusting in God to do the right thing, even if it is different than what we are praying for. Faith is trusting in God's ability to answer prayer so that He receives honor and glory. Sometimes that means that God will say no when we really want Him to say yes. For example, if a lot of people will come to know Jesus because someone we know is sick—and their life is a witness to the Lord through their sickness—God may choose to allow the illness to remain. These are very hard times, but these are the times God teaches us and helps us to grow as Christians.

When we pray with hearts that truly want God to be glorified, we will seek to pray prayers that line up with God's will, even when it's not what we want. Prayer is not for the purpose of getting what we want but what God wants. It's not "our will be done"; it's "Your will be done." Remember, even Jesus prayed that He wouldn't have to go to the cross, but He obediently yielded His will to the will of His Father—our Father! Because Jesus prayed for His Father's will to be done, we have been rescued from the penalty of our sin!

## ⮑ *Wrestling in prayer*

Think of a wrestling match. Especially if there are boys in your household, as there have always been in mine, it probably occurs on a regular basis. Two opponents put out a lot of effort to be declared the winner. Sometimes it feels like we must put forth a lot of effort in prayer before we see an answer. Sometimes we will not see the answer until we get to heaven, so we need to have complete faith that God has responded.

**Read:** Colossians 4:12

Is there a particularly heavy prayer need on your hearts today? Why not try "wrestling" in prayer! Spend an extra amount of time focusing on that particular prayer issue. Maybe it will be for an unsaved family member or for a people group that needs to hear the gospel of Christ. Focus in prayer on this issue until you sense a release from the Lord to stop. You may feel that you need to pray for many days in a row—sometimes even weeks or months or even years! Don't give up! God is faithful!

### ➲ Silent prayer

**Say:** Did you know that God is perfectly capable of hearing our thoughts when we pray silently? Even if we never open our mouths but only think our prayers to the Lord, He always knows what we are asking. There are times when it is not appropriate to pray out loud, or when we are unable to. Isn't it great that we can still communicate to God silently when we need to?

That's exactly what Hannah did. Do you remember reading about Hannah back in Step Three?

Sometimes it is hard to pray out loud. Some people are very shy. Other times, you may not be in a place where praying out loud is appropriate. There are many times when silent prayer is *needed!* We need to learn to be comfortable with silence. Sometimes in silence we hear the Lord more clearly (read Psalm 4:4)!

Give each family member an opportunity to spend some time in silent prayer. Here is a sample format you can use:

**Say:** I want everyone to think of two things about the Lord that make Him so great. Quietly tell Him from your heart why He is great. (Give them about thirty seconds between each section.) Think about anything you have done this week to make God sad. Confess it to Him and ask for His forgiveness. (Pause) Now, think of something you are thankful for. Tell God about it and thank Him. (Pause) Ask the Lord to bring to your mind one person who needs to know Him. Pray for that person. (Pause) Pray for a need that someone in this family may have right now. (Pause) The fruit of the Spirit is love, joy, peace, patience, kindness, goodness, faithfulness, gentleness, and self-control. Choose one of these areas and ask the Lord to help you to develop it in your life. (Pause)

You will need to guide young children at first. The best way is to team up with the youngest kids—or have older children pray with them. They will catch on quickly.

Talk about how important it is to have times of silence. Talking with God is a two-way street. We have to allow God an opportunity to speak to us too! As a family, spend some time in silence before God each day. Sit silently during this time . . . just focus on Christ (picture Him in your minds). Close your eyes if necessary. Ask God to speak to your hearts and just be silent before Him. Take at least one to two minutes, depending on the ages of your children. Then talk about the experience. What was it like to be quiet for such a long time? Did you feel close to Jesus when you focused on Him? Did He speak to your heart in any way?

### ➲ Praying in a loud voice

### 📄 MATERIALS NEEDED:

➲ Branches (real ones or branches made from green construction paper)

➲ Scissors

➲ Pencils

Sometimes it is appropriate to lift our voices to the Lord. Jesus modeled this upon the cross, when He cried out to God. Read Matthew 27:46; Luke 23:44–46; and Hebrews 5:7.

It is certainly appropriate to cry out to the Lord in times of desperate prayer. It is also appropriate to raise our voices in praise! Read Luke 17:15–16; 19:37–38; and Acts 4:23–24. Some shouted praise to Jesus. Read: John 12:12–13. If you have young children, why not act out this scene? Get some branches (or make your own out of green construction paper).

**Read:** "The next day the great crowd that had come for the Feast heard that Jesus was on his way to Jerusalem. They took palm branches and went out to meet him, shouting (begin waving the branches and shouting together): "Hosanna!" "Blessed is he who comes in the name of the Lord!" "Blessed is the King of Israel!"

Try praising God in a loud voice, saying Acts 4:24: "Sovereign Lord . . . you made the heaven and the earth and the sea, and everything in them." Find some other praises to speak loudly to Him.

**Hint:** Look in the Psalms!

You can pray loudly as you cry out for the nations to come to the Lord: Psalms 47:1; 57:9; 67:4; 86:9–10; 96:3–4; 99:2–3; 105:1; 108:3–4; 117:1–2; Isaiah 12:4. There are many more!

It is also appropriate to cry out to the Lord for revival! "Will you not revive us again, that your people may rejoice in you?" (Psalm 85:6)

✣

## HOW TO MAKE THIS
## A JOURNEY FOR A LIFETIME

1. Consistently practice what you have learned by taking the Side Trips for this journey and integrating them into your everyday prayer lives. You will have many opportunities to stretch and grow in your prayer lives as you "pray continually" (1 Thessalonians 5:17).

2. Find a special place to have your quiet time each day. It will be the place where you will meet with God, so choose it carefully. This place will change depending on where you are living throughout your life. Sometimes, you might want to have an indoor quiet place and an outdoor quiet place. Be sure to find somewhere that you can be alone and where you will not be interrupted. It doesn't have to be a fancy place or very big (remember, this is your prayer closet). You may want to have a basket or shelf where you keep your Bible, a journal, and any other materials that you wish to use. Consider having a tape or CD player there to spend some time in worship before the Lord. Wherever you choose to have your quiet time with the Lord, ask Him to set the place apart for your time together.

**Interesting Note:** Susannah Wesley, mother of Charles and John Wesley, two powerful evangelists from England, had so many children that for a season of her life her quiet time was held while she sat on a kitchen stool with her apron over her head.

3. As you pray, consider how you feel. If you are joyful, you may wish to stand with your hands raised to the Lord. If you are needing to cry out to God in repentance or on behalf of someone else, you may want to lie prostrate (facedown on the floor) before Him. If you are sensing the awesomeness of the Lord God Almighty, you may fall to your knees before Him. As you allow the Holy Spirit to prompt you, honor God with your body as well as your words. "Humble yourselves before the Lord, and he will lift you up" (James 4:10). Remember, there are times when you will want to cry out to the Lord and times you will feel the need to be quiet

before Him. Take time to listen so that He can speak to your heart: "Be still, and know that I am God" (Psalm 46:10a).

# Prayer Commands in Scripture

*The end of all things is near.*
*Therefore be clear minded and*
*self-controlled so that you can pray.*

1 PETER 4:7

When I ask my son David to mow the yard or take out the trash, he knows that these are not just suggestions. Even though I ask him nicely, he knows that if he doesn't do what I ask, there will be consequences. Fortunately, he is a pretty wise teenager and realizes that he should treat my request as a command, not a suggestion. That is how we need to look at the things God asks us to do in His Word. We need to make sure that we are being obedient to everything He asks us to do. When He commands us to do something, it is very clear.

When I began to journal (write down) many of my prayers, I always tried to study Scripture in such a way that I would have a personal application for my own life. I would ask, "What is God saying to me personally through His Word?" This proved to be an eye-opening experience as I started to see how many things I have treated lightly but that are actually commands from the very lips of Jesus! On this journey, you will learn what God's Word commands about prayer—and a few "shoulds" as well. If God's Word says we "should" do something, that's enough for me—how about you?

One very important thing I learned about prayer through studying the commands of God is that He commands . . . and I don't. What I mean is, God knows His perfect plan and purposes for my life and the life of my family. Sometimes that means that my prayers will not be answered with a yes. Did you know that God always answers our prayers but not always the way we "want" or "expect" Him to? Sometimes God answers my prayers with a "No" or with a "Wait" because He has something to teach me or because He wants to protect me . . . and always because He knows what is best. My job is to trust God and to always try to pray God's will and not my own. What I want is not always right or best!

As you read later in this journey about Jesus' prayers in the Garden of Gethsemane, you will see that even God's own Son didn't get the answer He hoped to have from His Father. He didn't want to die on the cross. But Jesus' example to us is in His perfect obedience to and faith in God's will when He prayed, "Not as I will, but as you will."

Parents, it is very important that children understand that there is no "magic formula" to prayer. It is also important that you teach them to stretch and grow towards praying God's will instead of their own. Sometimes they may not understand why God answers prayers a certain way . . . just like adults don't always understand. But you are raising up a praying family that needs to learn to trust that God's will is always, without exception, the very best for us . . . and brings Him the honor and glory He deserves.

Encourage your children to pray faith-filled prayers, without doubt—as they also seek to pray what God's will is in certain situations or for people they are interceding for. Also teach them to trust that God will answer these prayers of faith in the very best way—even though His answers may be hard sometimes. Just like we, as parents, don't always say yes to our children, we still try to give them the very best—and God's best is much better than ours could ever be.

# WHAT YOUR FAMILY WILL DISCOVER ON THIS JOURNEY

➤ *What God's Word commands about prayer*

➤ *It is important to practice and obey (do) the Word*

➤ *It is important to learn some Scripture passages on prayer well enough so that they will be "hidden in your heart" (Psalm 119:11)*

➤ *How God blesses your family as you are obedient to His Word*

➤ *How to pray God's will instead of your own*

 MEMORY VERSE:

1 Peter 4:7

**STEP ONE**  📖 Practice your memory verse

➲ *God's instructions on prayer*

**Say:** God gives us very clear instructions about how we are to pray.

**Read:** Matthew 6:5 (Remember—a parent does not always have to do the reading.)

**Ask:** What is a hypocrite? (Remember to give time for answers.)

• A phony person

• The Pharisees were hypocrites, and these are the people Jesus was talking about in Matthew 6:5.

**Ask:** How does Jesus tell us to pray in this passage of Scripture?

• Go to our room, close the door, and pray to the Father, who is unseen.

• Do not keep babbling—speak to God from your heart, not with words you think He wants to hear.

**Ask:** If God already knows what we need before we ask, why should we pray?
• Because God *wants* us to ask! He has chosen, to a great extent, to limit the working of His power to the prayers of His people. So, even if God knows what we want or need, He is generally not going to answer a prayer that is never prayed. Since God tells us *how* we should and shouldn't pray, we can assume that He *intends* for us to pray!

**Read:** Jude 1:20 and Ephesians 6:17–18
**Ask:** How are we told to pray in these passages?
• In the Holy Spirit

• On all occasions

• With all kinds of prayers and requests

• For all believers

**Ask:** What does it mean to pray in the Holy Spirit?
• It means to pray when the Spirit prompts us (moves us) and with the power of the Spirit. It is when we pray but depend upon the Spirit to give us the words. That takes faith on our part.

**Read:** Romans 8:26–27
**Ask:** How does the Holy Spirit help us when we pray?
• When we don't know how to pray or what to pray for, He intercedes for us.

• The Spirit intercedes in agreement with God's will (the Spirit is 100 percent informed of God's will—are we?).

• Sometimes we need the Spirit to express through us what we can't express in our own human strength or understanding. Remember, "The Spirit helps us in our weakness."

**Read:** James 1:6–7
**Ask:** When we pray, we must do what?
• Believe and not doubt.

**Ask:** Why is it important to believe when we pray?
• If we ask God to do something and then don't believe He can do it, there is no purpose to our prayer other than speaking words. We should not think that we will receive anything from the Lord in this case.

• There is no point to prayer if we do not believe that God has the ability to answer—even if it is not the answer we are expecting or wanting.

• We don't want to be double minded—or like a boat blown about in a sea of indecision. (You can illustrate this by using a toy boat or a paper boat in the sink or a bath tub. Have everyone blow on the boat at the same time . . . and show how it just doesn't know which way to go.)

**STEP TWO** 📖 Say your memory verse
➲ *Review the prayer commands we have learned*

• The purpose of prayer is meeting with God—not being seen by others.

Have each family member "hide" somewhere in the house. Set a timer for two minutes. Each person should spend that time praying to God where he can't be seen by others. Come back together when the timer goes off.

• We should speak to God from our hearts—not with words we think He wants to hear.

## Side Trip

Have each person (pair up a prereader with an older sibling or parent) spend five minutes quietly listening and focusing on God. Instruct them to read one of the Psalms or another passage in the Bible and meditate on what they have read. Have them ask the question, "Lord, what do You have for me in this passage?"

When the time is up, have a prayer time together. Ask that each person pray whatever God has placed on his or her heart.

• Pray in the Holy Spirit.

• Pray in the Spirit on all occasions with all kinds of prayers and requests.

## Side Trip

Instruct family members to keep track of times when they don't know how to pray. They can write these down in Journey Journals. Tell them to spend some time seeking the wisdom of the Holy Spirit. Write down what happens. Did they pray? Did they groan? Did they feel an assurance that the Holy Spirit was on the job? Share that each person's experience will probably be different than another's.

**Ask:** What have we learned about the Holy Spirit's role in prayer?

• Always keep on praying for all the saints.

## 🌲 Side Trip

Try to pray for people whenever they come to mind. Sometimes God will bring them to mind in the middle of the night. If you are awake, take a few minutes to pray for the person or situation on your heart. Sometimes God will bring a person to mind while you are driving in the car, taking a shower, or reading a book. We need to be ready to respond in prayer whenever we sense that God has given us a "prayer assignment." We never know when someone is needing prayer at the very moment God is prompting us to pray. That's why it is so important to be ready! Share your experiences with one another after several days of praying for people as they come to mind.

• When we pray, we must believe and not doubt.

## 🌲 Side Trip

Go outside, if possible. Otherwise, find a large room. Have each person close his or her eyes one at a time. Tell the person to picture where he or she is in the yard or room, and to try to think about where he or she is going as you give directions. Give the person three or four specific directions, such as: take five big steps forward, go to the right three steps, take one very small step backwards. Ask the person to tell you where he or she is. Have the person open his or her eyes to see how close his or her guess was. Now, have the other members of the family do the same.

Next, have each person close his or her eyes and imagine that he or she is being blown around by the wind. (The rest of you can even make noises like a blowing wind, if you wish.) The person should hold out his or her arms and be blown around the room or yard by the "wind" for several seconds. Have other family members spin the person around and push them gently in different directions. Tell the person to stop and guess where in the room or yard they are. Have the person open his or her eyes to see where he or she ended up. Then, do the same thing with the next family member until everyone has had a turn. Be careful that no one bumps into anyone else.

Remind your family that this is what it is like when we doubt instead of believe. We can end up somewhere completely different than we thought or have no control over where we go. But when we believe, and listen to God's voice, He will tell us exactly where to go and what to do.

**STEP THREE**  📖 Say your memory verse

**Read:** Matthew 6:9–13

**Ask:** What did the disciples ask Jesus to do?

• They asked Him to teach them to pray.

**Ask:** How did Jesus teach the disciples (and us) to pray?

• We should recognize that God is our Father in heaven.

• We should hallow (give honor to) the name of our Father in heaven.

• We should pray for His kingdom to come.

• We should pray for His will to be done on earth as it is in heaven.

• We should ask for our daily bread.

• We should ask for forgiveness for our sins and be forgiving of those who sin against us.

• We should pray that we won't be tempted.

• We should pray to be delivered (protected) from the evil one.

**Pray** the Lord's Prayer (Disciples' Prayer) together in stages:
• Give Him honor—spend some time praising Him (You can use "Lord, You are _____" from Journey #4).

• Pray for His kingdom to come and for His will to be done on earth as it is in heaven.

• Ask for the things you need individually and as a family.

• Spend some time in silent prayer asking forgiveness for anything you have done that has made God sad (sin).

• Continue in silent prayer as you forgive those who have sinned against you in some way.

• Think of at least one thing that makes God sad, and has been hard for you to keep from doing. Pray that God will give you the strength to keep from doing this sin, and that you won't be tempted to do wrong things.

• Pray that the Lord will protect your family from the enemy.

**STEP FOUR** 📖 Say your memory verse

➲ *We need to have a continuous prayer connection with the Lord.*

**Read:** Psalm 105:4, Isaiah 55:6, Ephesians 6:18, 1 Thessalonians 5:17

**Ask:** What commands are we given in these Scriptures that tell us to pray? (Allow plenty of time for your family members to answer first.)

• We are to look to the Lord and His strength, seeking His face always. (How do we seek His face? In prayer.)

• We are to seek the Lord while He may be found and call on Him while He is near. (Since Christ lives in us if we are Christians, is there ever a time when He is not near?)

• We are to pray in the Spirit on all occasions with all kinds of prayers and requests.

• We are to be alert.

• We are to always keep on praying for all the saints.

• Pray continually.

**Ask:** In Ephesians 6:18, the Scripture tells us to be alert. Why?

• This is a reminder that we are always in a spiritual battle against the devil that must be fought in God's strength and not our own. If we are not alert, the Enemy can catch us unaware and we will not be ready. The Enemy will use our weaknesses against us to cause us to sin against God and others.

**Encouragement:**
**Read:** 1 John 3:21–24
**Ask:** How can we have confidence before God and receive from Him anything we ask?

• When our hearts do not condemn us (we are free from sin).

• When we obey God's commands and do what pleases Him.

**Ask:** What happens if we are obedient to His commands?

• We live in Him and He lives in us.

**Ask:** How do we know that He lives in us?

• By the Spirit He gave us—to be our teacher, and to help us to keep that close connection with God through prayer.

## 🏕 Side Trip

Fill the bathtub with enough water to allow something to float. Find a rubber duck, a boat, or something that will float and tie a string to it in some way. Have one child (you can take turns with others) move the object around in the bathtub by manipulating the string. Talk about how it goes where we want it to because it is connected to the string. Now, cut or remove the string. Make a few waves in the tub and watch the object float around aimlessly. Discuss how that is like our prayer life. As long as we are connected to God through prayer, we can obediently say, go and do what He directs us to. When we aren't connected, we aren't in contact with God. Sometimes we will say, go and do things we shouldn't and lose our way. (It may seem as though this book has used too many ways to get this same concept across—but it has been reinforced because it is so very important to understand clearly and without question.)

**Read:** John 15:5

**Ask:** Why is it important to stay attached to the Vine (God)?

• Because if we don't, we can do nothing!

**STEP FIVE** 📖 Say your memory verse

➲ *We are to give thanks to the Lord in prayer.*

**Read:** 1 Chronicles 16:8 and Isaiah 12:4

**Ask:** In these two passages, what does God's Word say we are to do?

- Give thanks to the Lord.

- Call upon His name.

- Make known among the nations what He has done.

- Proclaim that His name is exalted.


**Ask:** How can we express our thanks to God for His goodness to us in these ways?

**Ideas:**

- Tell others when we are thankful and let them know what God has done.

- Pray (call upon His name).

- Give Him thanks personally.

- Take part in a missions project that is bringing the Good News of Jesus to people in another part of the world or even in our own nation. You can do this by:

    ➲ Going on a missions trip yourself.

    ➲ Providing financial and/or prayer support for others to go.

**Read:** 1 Thessalonians 5:18

**Ask:** For younger children—or just to make things clearer: What are circumstances? (Things that happen to us—they can be good or bad. For example, when you are on a winning team, these are good circumstances. When you have been injured and can't play on the team, you are in bad circumstances. The good thing is that Jesus is Lord over all of our circumstances, and He can work through them—good or bad, to bring honor and glory to Himself.)

**Ask:** What is different about this passage when compared to the first two you read?

- We are to give thanks in all of the circumstances that come into our lives—good or bad, because this is God's will for us in Christ Jesus.

**Ask:** What do you think about that? Is it always easy to give thanks? Why do you think God wants us to be thankful even in circumstances that aren't the best?

- Because He wants us to trust in Him—no matter what. God can do amazing things through all of our circumstances—even the bad or unpleasant ones.

- Sometimes He has something important to teach us through our bad circumstances.

**Ask:** What kinds of things can God teach us through bad circumstances? Can you think of an example in your life or in the life of someone you know?

**Pray:** Let's ask God to help us to be truly thankful and to give thanks to Him in prayer and praise in the midst of all of our circumstances. Take time to pray. Now, let's ask God to help us to learn how to exalt His name and to make known among the nations (even our own nation) what He has done. Take time to pray.

## STEP SIX 📖 Say your memory verse

*Sometimes we are commanded to pray for people who have been unkind to us in some way.*

**Read:** Matthew 5:43 and Luke 6:27

**Ask:** What does the Lord ask us to do?

• Love our enemies

• Pray for those who persecute us so that we may be sons (and daughters) of our Father in heaven.

• We are to do good to those who hate us.

• We are to bless those who curse us.

• We are to pray for those who mistreat us.

**Ask:** Why does God want us to do these things?

• Because "He causes His sun to rise on the evil and the good, and sends rain on the righteous and the unrighteous" (1 Timothy 2:3–4). In other words, He loves *everyone* on this planet, good or bad. Remember: God wants everyone to be saved!

**Ask:** Why is what God is asking us to do very different from what our culture tells us to do?

• Our culture tells us to love those who love us and to hate our enemies.

**Ask:** Is praying for those who are unkind to us an easy thing to do? Why or why not? Can you give an example in your life? Can anyone tell of a time when he prayed for someone who had been unkind? What happened?

**Comment:** Sometimes, praying for that person can change us instead of him. Have you ever had that happen?

**Ask:** What is the reward for doing what God tells us to do?

• We will be sons (and daughters) of our Father in heaven.

• We will be acting like Jesus—doing what He would do.

**Pray:** Ask the Lord to help us pray for those who are not nice to us. Ask Him to help us love others as much as He loves them.

## 🌲 Side Trip

What are some things we could do as a family to show love to those who persecute us? Let's make a list and see how many we can do in the next few days.

**Story:** A friend of mine told a story of a next-door neighbor who was unkind to her kids. Instead of getting upset or angry, the family prayed for her, asking God's blessing upon her, and praying that she would come to know Jesus. They began to do "random acts of kindness" for her. They took her cookies and shoveled her walk. Gradually, the ice between the fence began to melt and the unkind person (who was really just unhappy and lonely) began to respond to their love. Now they have become good friends and better neighbors. Do you have a situation like this one? Maybe there is a child who has been unkind to you at school. Pray earnestly for him and his family. It could be circumstances in his family that cause him to behave the way he does. How could you and your family show love to him?

Practice praying for unkind people. Whenever you see someone mistreating others, even if it doesn't involve you or your family, be sure to pray for them. Find ways to share the love of Christ with him. Perhaps you could pray for people in prison or jail. Prison chaplains will be happy to give you and your family the names of people to pray for.

**STEP SEVEN** 📖 Say your memory verse

➲ *God simply commands us to call, seek, ask, and knock. He promises good things to those who are obedient in prayer.*

**Read:** Luke 11:9–10

**Ask:** What does God command us to do? And what are His promises if we obey?

• Ask—It will be given to us.

• Seek—We will find what we are seeking.

• Knock—The door will be opened to us (we will receive what God has for us).

**Let's imagine:**

Pretend we are outside in the middle of winter. We are very cold and hungry, and we have been searching for a long time to find someone to help us. Now, imagine that we come upon a big house and that we can see through the window. There is a big fire in the fireplace and a large table covered with food. If we just stand outside and wish we could go in, but do nothing, we will probably stay just the way we are.

What if we knew that all we have to do is knock and the door will open—and we can go in and get warm and be fed? Wouldn't we do that right away? God wants to give us what we need—if we will be obedient and ask, seek, and knock. Sometimes some wonderful other things happen as well that go beyond our needs. God can be very abundant in how He chooses to bless as we are faithful to ask. Sometimes God blesses us beyond what we deserve. Maybe He would choose to have a warm bubble bath ready for us in this big house. Or, maybe there is a delicious dessert on the table of food that we didn't see before.

**Ask:** What should we do as God gives us blessings?

• Thank Him.

• Look for ways to bless others as we have been blessed.

**Read:** Jeremiah 33:3

**Ask:** What does God command us to do?
• Call to Him (pray).

**Ask:** What will God do if we call to Him?
• He will answer us and tell us great and unsearchable things we do not know.

**Read:** John 16:24
**Ask:** What will God do when we are obedient to ask in His name?

• We will receive what we ask for.

• Our joy will be complete (perfect or fulfilled).

**Read:** Psalm 2:8
**Ask:** What will God do when we ask of Him?
• He will make the nations Christ's inheritance through us.

• He will make the ends of the earth Christ's possession through us.

**Discussion:** This is a missions prayer. As we pray for peoples and the nations, we should ask that God the Father will give them to Jesus as His inheritance (gift from God). It is our job to ask for the salvation of those who don't know Christ. I have wondered if anyone comes to Jesus Christ without first having been prayed for. What if there are people in your lives, as well as people around the world who will never know Jesus apart from your prayers? If you knew that, wouldn't you continually be praying for others? Maybe you need to be praying for the Lord of the harvest to send workers into His harvest field (Matthew 9:38). (See Journey # 9, "Prayer Missionaries.")

**STEP EIGHT**  📖 Say your memory verse

➲ *Sometimes the Lord tells us to pray for something very specific.*

**Read:** Psalm 122:6

**Ask:** What does the Word tell us to do?

• Pray for the peace of Jerusalem.

**Ask:** How can we do this?

• If you want some specific prayers: go to this Web site: http://blessings.org/si/jerusalem.html

## 🌲 *Side Trip*

Find out all of the information you can about Jerusalem. Why is Jerusalem so precious to God that He would specifically tell us to pray for it? There are many Web sites about praying for the peace of Jerusalem besides the one mentioned above. I found that the easiest way to see them all is to go to www.google.com and type this in the search: "Pray for the Peace of Jerusalem." You'll have a big selection to choose from for information.

**Read:** Zechariah 10:1

**Ask:** What does the Word tell us to do?

• Ask the Lord for rain in the springtime—we are to pray and trust the Lord for His provision because He is able!

**Read:** Psalm 32:6

**Ask:** What does the Word tell us to do?

• Pray to the Lord while He may be found so that we can be rescued from troubling or difficult circumstances.

**STEP NINE** 📖 Say your memory verse

➲ *God tells us to pray so that all men will come to the knowledge of the truth of Jesus.*

**Read:** Matthew 9:37–38

**Ask:** What does "the harvest is plentiful but the workers are few" mean?

• There are people needing Christ but not enough workers to reach them.

• There is work to be done but not enough workers to do it.

**Ask:** What is God asking us to do?

• He is asking us to pray to the Lord of the harvest (Jesus) so that workers will be sent to His harvest field.

• He may be asking us to be the answer to our own prayers—maybe we are the workers God is wanting to use and/or send to those who do not know Christ.

• Sometimes in our churches, we need to disciple or mentor (teach and train) others so that they can grow in Christ.

**Ask:** Where do we see the plentiful harvest right now? What can we do about it?

**Note:** Did you know that there is a place called the 10/40 Window where 98 percent of the unreached people live? Unreached people are those who have yet to hear about Jesus in any meaningful way and who have no church in their area capable of reaching them with the Good News. The 10/40 Window also has the smallest amount of missionaries working in it (about 2 percent). It extends from 10° degrees north of the equator and stretches from North Africa all the way across to China. For more information about the 10/40 Window, see the Resource section. Please pray that God will send workers into this very dark harvest field.

**Activity:** Draw a picture of the harvest field in Matthew 9:37–38.

**Discuss:** Talk about what you have drawn. Some may have drawn a field that looks ready to be harvested. Others may have drawn a picture of the world with lots of people stretching their hands out in need.

**Action Steps:** What are some things that need doing at your church that will help us reach the lost? How can our family help? Maybe we can pray for God to raise up just the right people for all of the things that need to be done. (Always remember that it might be *us*.) Is anyone at our church communicating regularly with every missionary family? Is someone sending them cards and encouraging notes and praying for them regularly? Does our church have some kind of outreach to the lost or to people who are searching for the truth, such as Lighthouses of Prayer or the Alpha Course? Maybe we could become a Lighthouse to pray for our neighbors (see Journey #1). Or maybe we could pray for those leading and attending a class for those seeking Christ.

**STEP TEN**  📖 Say your memory verse

➲ *God tells us to pray to guard against temptation.*

**Activity:** Before beginning your prayer journey time today, put out a box of donuts (with a clear lid) or some cookies—anything that can tempt your family—on the table where it will be in plain sight of everyone. Put a big note or sign on the box or plate that says, "Do Not Touch." Watch to see what family members do as they become aware of the tempting goodies. Mom and Dad (or an older child, if this is the person teaching the lesson today) should be nowhere to be seen for several minutes. Give everyone a chance to decide if he or she is going to do the right thing and leave the goodies alone. Then bring everyone together for a discussion.

**Discussion:** How did you feel when you saw the donuts? If you wanted to eat one, why didn't you? If you did eat one, how do you feel now? What was the right thing to do, and did you do it?

**Read:** Matthew 26:41 and Luke 22:39–40

**Ask:** These Scriptures tell us to do something very specific. What is it?
- "Watch and pray" and "Pray."

**Ask:** Why does God ask us to watch and pray?
- So that we will not fall into temptation.

**Ask:** What kind of temptation is Jesus talking about?
- The temptation to sin.

**Ask:** How can we be tempted to sin?
- Because even though our spirits might be willing to do the right thing, our bodies are weak. It is our bodies that cause us the problem.

**Ask:** What should we do about it?
- We need to pray for spiritual strength so that our bodies don't cause us to sin.

**Ask:** So, can prayer keep us from temptation and sin?
- *Yes!*

**Ask:** So, when we are feeling tempted, what should we do?
• *Pray!*

**Discussion:** If Jesus needed to tell His own disciples to watch and pray, how much more do we need to? Have you ever been tempted to do or say the wrong thing? (If the donuts sitting in front of them don't help, give an example.) Do you think that stopping to pray about it would have helped you to make a better decision? Why or why not? What are some things that tempt you now? Think about what can you do so that you won't be tempted. (Have each person share one way in which he or she is tempted.)

**Pray:** Let's pray that we will all "watch and pray" so that we won't be so easily led to be tempted. We can also be helpful to each other. When one of us is tempted we can pray for or with that person.

## STEP ELEVEN  📖 Say your memory verse

**Read:** James 1:5–8
**Ask:** What does verse 5 say we should do?
• If we lack wisdom, we should ask God.

**Ask:** What will God do when we ask?
• He will give generously to all without finding fault and will give us wisdom.

**Ask:** In verse 6, how does God say we are to ask?
• We must believe and not doubt.

**Ask:** Why should we believe and not doubt when we pray?
• Because if we don't believe, we don't have faith that God can or will answer.

**Ask:** Is there any point to prayer if we don't believe that God can or will answer?

- There is no point to prayer if we don't believe that—because we can't have it both ways! God answers the prayers that are prayed from a heart that believes He can answer. Even many people who don't know Jesus as Savior and Lord still believe that God can answer their prayers. Sometimes God chooses to reveal Jesus to them through these prayers. Think of it this way: The believer prays with faith, knowing that God is able to answer prayer. The unbeliever does not have this faith. He prays hoping that God will answer.

**Ask:** What is the prayer command in this passage?

- Therefore confess your sins to one another and pray for each other so that you may be healed.

**Encouragement:** The prayer of a righteous man (or woman or child) is powerful and effective!

**Read:** James 5:13–16

**Ask:** When should we pray?

- When we are in trouble!

**Ask:** What should we do when we are happy?

- We should sing praises (should pray; should praise). When things are going well, we need to praise God. Praise is prayer too! We are adoring and thanking the Lord for who He is and what He has done!

**Ask:** What has God done lately for you or for the family that you can praise Him for?

- Spend some time sharing what the Lord has done.

- Give praise to God!

**Ask:** What should we do when we are sick?
• We should call the elders of the church to pray over us and anoint us with oil in the name of the Lord.

**Ask:** Why should we do this?
• Because the prayer offered in faith will make the sick person well, the Lord will raise him up, and if he has sinned, he will be forgiven.

**Discuss:** This is another example of "should pray" combined with a prayer command.
**Ask:** What is the command?
• Therefore confess your sins to each other and pray for each other so that you may be healed.

**Encouragement:** The prayer of a righteous man (or woman or child) is powerful and effective!

⤳

## HOW TO MAKE THIS
## A JOURNEY FOR A LIFETIME

1. As you read Scripture, always be looking for the Lord's prayer commands. Do what He says.

2. Believe that the Lord hears and answers your prayers. Encourage others by sharing what God has done in your life through answered prayer.

3. As you read and study the Word of God, always be looking for what He is trying to say to you personally. Ask Him to show you how to respond.

4. Keeping a journal is a good way to keep track of what you learn and how you are growing in Christ.

PART 3

# PRAYING
# FOR OTHERS

# The Needs
# of Others

*I urge, then, first of all,*
*that requests, prayers, intercession*
*and thanksgiving be made for everyone.*

1 TIMOTHY 2:1

When our sons were younger, it was natural to hear their prayers be rather self-centered. As they grew in their awareness of the purposes of prayer, they learned that there were many other things on God's heart besides their own personal needs and wants. God wants us to pray about the things we need—and even the things we want if they are in line with His will. However, He also wants us to pray beyond ourselves—for others. This is called *intercession*. Intercession is prayer that focuses on other people and on situations other than our own. We are all called to be intercessors, although some people are especially gifted in that area. You probably could name several people who are known as the "prayer warriors" at your church. As we pray on behalf of others, we are asking God to get involved in their lives and situations. We must always be ready, however, to be willing to be the answer to our own prayers, if God calls us to be.

I remember when this hit home. As I was praying (interceding) for a friend with a financial need, the Lord placed it very clearly on my heart that I was to be the source of meeting her need. I questioned God (silly me) at first, being quite sure that I was not hearing correctly. The more I questioned it, the more strongly I felt urged to respond to her need. So I tried being obedient and left an anonymous gift in an envelope on the front seat of my friend's car. The next time I saw her, she was so filled with joy and faith because God had answered her prayer for grocery money—to the exact dollar of her need. Wow! Was my faith ever built up—and did I ever learn an important lesson about intercession. Sometimes (but not always) when we are called to pray for the needs of another, God will use *us* to be the answer to our own prayer!

## WHAT YOUR FAMILY WILL DISCOVER ON THIS JOURNEY

➤ *The meaning of the word* intercession

➤ *How to be sensitive to and aware of the needs of those around you—friends, family, churches, organizations, neighbors*

➤ *How to pray for those needs*

➤ *How to listen so that you can be the answer to your own prayers (responding to the needs as the Lord leads you)*

 MEMORY VERSE:

*1 Timothy 2:1*

**STEP ONE** 📖 Practice your memory verse
  ➲ *What is intercession?*

  **Ask:** What is intercession? (Wait for responses.)
  **Teaching:** Intercession is praying for other people and for situations other than our own. It is coming to God on behalf of others.
  **Ask:** How has God blessed each of us individually? How has God blessed us as a family? (Share your answers.)

**Say:** Sometimes when we are more aware of the blessings of God in our lives, we can see the needs of others more clearly.

**Ask:** Has our family ever gone through a hard time? (Give time for responses. Be ready to supply some examples of difficult things you have gone through together.) What was it like for you? Maybe you are going through a difficult time right now. How has your trust in God helped you in the past or how is it helping you now? Do you believe that He has the way to help you meet your need?

**Share:** Have each person in the family share one need he has. It can be a physical, emotional, or spiritual need.

**Pray** for one another. Ask God to meet these needs. Write down the names of one to three people who have at least one need you could pray about or get a list of prayer needs from your church. Spend some time praying for them right now.


## STEP TWO 📖 Say your memory verse

➲ *Helping others*


**Read:** Luke 11:5–8

**Ask:** What did the hungry friend need? Who had the bread? Who brought the hungry friend together with the friend who had bread so that the hungry friend's need could be met?

**Say:** This is a good picture of intercession: One friend connects a friend in need with the one who can meet that need. When we pray for someone else, we connect him or her to God, who can meet his or her need.

**Read:** Matthew 25:34–40.

**Discuss** some of the experiences you have had in helping others.

**Ask:** How would it change our lives if we met the needs of other people as if each one of them were Jesus Christ Himself? Would it make a difference in how we looked at others? Would it help us pray for them better? Would it help us meet their needs?

**Pray and listen:** Spend some time in silent prayer and then spend some time just opening up your heart to hear what the Lord might have to say to you.

**Share** with one another anything you sense the Lord is placing on your hearts to do.

## STEP THREE ᵚ Say your memory verse
➔ *Listing needs in your community*

**Write** down some of the needs you see in your community —homeless people, littered streets, crisis-pregnancy centers, food banks, hospitals.

**Pray** for each area that comes to mind. As you pray, be aware that the Lord will probably stir you into action!

**Discuss:** Is there one project or ministry your family could adopt for prayer? How could prayer lead you into action?

## STEP FOUR ᵚ Say your memory verse
➔ *"Adopting" an official*

**Read:** Titus 3:13–14

**Adopt** an official in your city—the mayor, the chief of police, the street commissioner.

**Pray** for him or her today and continue on a daily basis. Decide as a family how long you want to do this. The Lord may lay this person on your heart for a long time or for a short time.

**Write:** Let him know that your family is praying for him. Send a note or a Prayer-A-Gram or drop by for a visit.

**Ask** him if there is anything specific you could be praying about for your community and for him and his family. Be faithful to pray for your "adopted" official.

## STEP FIVE 📖 Say your memory verse
➲ *How God views our helping others*

**Read:** Isaiah 58:10–11

**Ask:** Does praying for and helping others mean as much to you as it does to God? Why or why not? If you satisfy the needs of others, what will God do? If you find that you could improve in this area, talk about some things you could do. How could you help each other to be more aware of the needs around you?

**Pray:** Continue to pray for the people whose name(s) you wrote down, for the prayer needs of your church, for your adopted ministry, and for your city official.

## 📍 *Side Trips*
➲ *Prayer basket/Answer basket*

Place two small baskets in a central place in your home. Whenever you learn of a need, write it down and put it into the prayer basket. At mealtimes or other times determined by your family, pray for these needs. Whenever an answer comes, put it into the answer basket. Be sure to celebrate the answered prayer with someone!

### ➲ *Driving*

When you come across an accident, a homeless person, or a home that has been burned—pray! Right then! Ask the Lord to show you how to respond to the needs.

### ➲ Compassion International or World Vision child

If you support a child through Compassion International, World Vision, or a similar group, you can pray specifically for him or his family. It would be a good idea to pray also for his village or city, people group, and nation.

### ➲ Web site

Start a family Web site where you take prayer requests from other families. Offer to pray for them regularly. Encourage others to go to your Web site to pray for the needs too.

### ➲ Family prayer calendar

### 📑 MATERIALS NEEDED:

➲ A dry-erase calendar (you can purchase one from any office supply store) or a calendar made on the computer

1. Generate prayer requests for each day of the month for the upcoming month. Keep a separate list of all requests so that you can see how God is moving. Pray as a family for the requests on this calendar each day.

2. You can make a praise calendar, also, to record the answered prayers!

3. Once a month, generate a calendar to send to family and friends that pray for you. Decorate it with pictures (photos and drawings).

✍

# HOW TO MAKE THIS
# A JOURNEY FOR A LIFETIME

1. *Look around you!* There are needs everywhere—even in your very own church! Keep the eyes and ears of your hearts open to see and hear what God wants you to pray about and what He would have you do.

2. Interceding for others can become as natural as breathing if you will keep the eyes and ears of your spirit open to the Holy Spirit at all times. Whenever you are filled with compassion or even get upset over the actions of others, become a prayer warrior for the people and/or situations involved. Don't criticize or worry— pray! Remember, God may want to use you to be the answer to your own prayers.

3. Let people know when you are praying for them, if possible. You can tell them in person, call them, or send a note. You can even pray for people you don't know. Knowing that others care enough to pray can make a big difference in the lives of many people. Your prayers may be exactly what is needed to bring comfort and peace into people's lives. Let God use you!

4. Be creative as you intercede for others. Maybe your family can become a Lighthouse of Prayer (see Journey #1). Or you might wish to prayerwalk as a family around your neighborhood, around your church or school, or through downtown. See Journey #10 for more information on Prayerwalking.

# Our Ten Most Wanted

*Andrew, Simon Peter's brother, was one of the two who heard what John had said and who had followed Jesus. The first thing Andrew did was to find his brother Simon and tell him, "We have found the Messiah." . . . And he brought him to Jesus.*

JOHN 1:40–42

For a long time, my youngest son wanted to be an FBI agent. He wanted to catch criminals and bring them to justice, to crack codes, and to follow the clues to track down those who brought harm to others. I remember always being intrigued by posters of people on the FBI's Most-Wanted List. Sometimes they would be in the post office; other times, their images appeared on television. When I was a child, it never occurred to me that praying for these people would be something that would please God. No matter what they have done, God still loves them and wants to draw them to Himself.

Have you ever wondered what God's Most-Wanted posters look like? I left out the "Ten" intentionally, because God would never limit His list! God's list has billions of pictures because He "wants *all* men to be saved and to come to a knowledge of the truth" (1 Timothy 2:4, emphasis mine).

It is my personal belief that people do not come to Christ unless someone (or many someones) has been praying for them. The prayers of God's people prepare the way for Him to work in the lives of others. I had the privilege of meeting the woman who prayed me into the kingdom of God. Her faithful prayers for me allowed the door of my heart to be opened so that I could receive Christ as my Lord and Savior. (Thank you, Clara Eggart—my life has borne fruit for God because you were faithful to pray when God placed me on your heart. Who knows how many thousands have and will continue to come to Him as a result of your prayers for me and others?)

As you will learn on this journey, praying for the lost—whether they are next door or across the ocean—is God's way to bring the lost to Himself. You could pray for hearts to be open and receptive in Albania, and as a result of your prayers, missionaries could find people ready to hear about Christ. You could pray for a relative and find that he or she is now more willing to listen than ever before. Prayer is God's chosen way to accomplish His will on this earth. Prayer prepares the way, prepares the people, and prepares the one who brings the Good News of Jesus. It is the most powerful tool for evangelism because it was not conceived in the mind of man but in the heart of God.

My prayer for our family and yours is that we would all be equally passionate about praying for those who are outside of the family of Christ. Fortunately, we don't have to track them down. God puts burdens for some on our hearts and brings others into our paths every day. Many of them are in our own families. May this journey continue until "this gospel of the kingdom will be preached in the whole world as a testimony to all nations, and then the end will come" (Matthew 24:14).

## WHAT YOUR FAMILY WILL DISCOVER ON THIS JOURNEY

➤ *How important it is to God that we pray for the lost in our own families, in our neighborhoods and cities, in our nation, and around the world*

➤ *How to prepare the way in prayer for people to hear the Good News of Jesus Christ*

➤ *How to pray effectively and specifically for the lost*

## 📖 MEMORY VERSES:

---

*1 Timothy 2:3–4*

**STEP ONE**  📖 Practice verses 3–4 (memory verses)
➲ *Starting a Ten Most-Wanted list*

**Read:** 1 Timothy 2:1–4 together.
**Ask:** What does God want?
• He wants *all* men (and women and children) to be saved and to come to a knowledge of the truth (to know Jesus).

**Activity:** Make a list of the ten people your family most urgently would like to see come to know Christ. You may wish to begin with unsaved family members and friends, then move to neighbors, classmates, and coworkers. Choose people who have some kind of relationship with your family, if possible. This will make the journey very exciting and personal. Write this list in your Journey Journals!

Now that you have made your Ten Most-Wanted list, do two things:

1. Read Mark 10:27 and make a commitment as a family to believe together that God can save each person on your list.

2. Read 1 Timothy 2:1–4 again and pray for each person, making his or her name known to God. Ask God for the salvation of each person.

**STEP TWO**  📖 Say your memory verses
➲ *Gathering information*

**Say together:** *It is God's will that all people should be saved!*

**Read** the following Scriptures together: Ezekiel 18:23; Matthew 18:14; 1 John 5:16; 2 Peter 3:9; 1 Timothy 2:3–4

Make an information sheet about each of your Ten Most Wanted. Include everything you know about each one—work, school, family. Be as thorough as possible so that you can pray specifically for each person.

## STEP THREE  📖 Say your memory verses

### ⮑ *Stumbling blocks*

**Say:** We have an enemy named Satan, who doesn't want everyone to know Jesus. In fact, the devil is going to do everything he can to stop this from happening. He is going to try to discourage us or distract us as we pray for these people to come to Christ. So we must be faithful and persistent (determined).

**Ask:** Why do some people have such a hard time even hearing about Jesus? (You may wish to write down some of the answers given. No doubt you have asked yourself this question many times if you have spent much time evangelizing.)

**Say:** Let's see what the Bible has to say about this!

In Scripture, it is very clear why some people are resistant to the gospel.

• Some of them have blinded eyes. Read 2 Corinthians 4:4.

• Until we accept Jesus Christ as Savior and Lord, we are set up against the plans of God. This puts us in a position against the Lord where the Enemy of our souls (the devil) has a greater freedom to manipulate us. Read Ephesians 2:2.

• Satan snatches the Word away! Read Matthew 13:4, 19.

**Say:** Because of these stumbling blocks set up by the Enemy to slow down our efforts at reaching those who need to know Christ, we need to do more than be prepared scripturally with a polished presentation of the gospel. It is just not enough to simply proclaim the message—we need to prepare in *prayer!*

**Pray** for the ten on your list, using the Scriptures above. Ask God to open blinded eyes. Ask Him to keep each person from being manipulated (used) by the Enemy. Ask the Lord to protect them from having the Word snatched away from their hearts.

## STEP FOUR 📖 Say your memory verses

➲ *Gathering pictures*

See how many pictures you can find of people on your Ten Most Wanted list. Draw pictures of those you don't have photographs of (you may need to put the name under the picture, in case you don't have any artists in your midst).

**Pray** that God will draw each person on your list to Himself. "No one can come to me unless the Father who sent me draws him, and I will raise him up at the last day" (John 6:44).

## STEP FIVE 📖 Say your memory verses

➲ *Sin in our lives*

**Say:** Today we are going to talk about how to pray about sin in the lives of our Ten Most Wanted. Before we do that, however, it is important to deal with sin in our own lives first. Take a few minutes to write down one or more things you would like to confess to God and ask forgiveness for. Maybe you said something unkind to your brother or sister. Maybe you were disrespectful to one of your parents. Maybe you have been angry with someone in the family. Now is the time to take care of these things. We can't pray for the sins of others until we deal with the sins in our own lives first.

**Read:** Luke 6:42 together and talk about it.

**Pray:** Take some time to pray silently together. Confess your sins to the Lord. (See Journey #3.)

**Read:** 2 Corinthians 5:17

**Say:** Now that we have confessed our own sins, let's pray against negative or sinful habits in the lives of our Ten Most Wanted.

**Pray** against the hold these habits have in their lives.

**Pray** that they will be convicted by the Holy Spirit to repent of these things and become a new creation in Christ.

If the person associates with people who affect his/her life negatively, pray for the breaking up of this influence/friendship/relationship that draws or keeps the person away from Christ. (Read 2 Corinthians 6:14.)

If there are certain activities that influence the person's life in a negative way, pray that they will be replaced with positive activities and/or that the negative influence becomes powerless. (Read Galatians 5:1.)

Pray that any negative experiences from the person's past will be healed in such a way that Christ's power is evident. (Read Romans 6:1–4.)

**STEP SIX** 📖 Say your memory verses

➲ *Note cards*

🗐 MATERIALS NEEDED:

⮑ Flashlight

⮑ Ten 3 x 5 cards

**Read:** 2 Corinthians 4:5–6

**Write** the name of a person from your list on each of the ten cards. Get a flashlight and go to a room that is dark. Shine the light on the name of each Ten Most Wanted person, one at a time. As you do, pray that God will reveal (show) Himself to that person so that he or she can see the light of Christ.

**Ask:** How can God do this? Through the life our family lives—our example; through the lives of others; through His Spirit in a supernatural way—maybe in a dream or vision; through the Word (Bible).

**Pray** that the Holy Spirit will bring just the right individual(s) into his or her life to speak about Christ (realizing that it might be *you*)!

**STEP SEVEN** 📖 Say your memory verses

⮑ *Listing new people to pray for*

Here is a way to expand your prayer outreach. Have each individual choose from three to five new people to begin praying for. Parents or older siblings may pair up with younger children for this. If you have four people in your family and you already have ten people to pray for as a family—and then, each of the four people chooses five more people—you are collectively now praying for thirty people! Think how the kingdom of God could expand if every family did this! Be sure to write down in your Journey Journals the names of those for whom you are praying and when each begins to take steps toward knowing Jesus. Celebrate when each comes to Christ! Continue to pray for them as they grow in their relationship with Him!

 *Side Trip*

➲ *Bookmarks*

📋 MATERIALS NEEDED:

➲ Heavy paper or cardboard cut into bookmark-sized strips

➲ Access to a laminating machine (or use clear contact paper)

➲ Optional: Pictures of the Ten Most Wanted (photocopies work!)

Write the names of the Ten Most Wanted on bookmark-sized paper or cardboard. If you can attach their pictures also, that's great! Laminate the bookmarks and keep them in your Bibles as a reminder to pray! Post bookmarks on mirrors, the refrigerator, and any other place where you are likely to see them during the day—these will serve as a reminder to pray.

❧

## HOW TO MAKE THIS
## A JOURNEY FOR A LIFETIME

1. Be faithful! George Müller prayed daily for a large group of men he knew to come to Christ. Over the

next several decades, he continued to pray for them by name as one by one they began to accept Jesus as Savior and Lord. He was blessed to see almost all of them saved. There were three men left when Müller died; however, one came to Christ upon hearing of Müller's death. The last two accepted Jesus the day of Müller's funeral. We will never know the impact of our prayers for the lost this side of heaven.

2. Remain faithful and pray continually for those the Lord lays upon your heart, whether they are relatives, neighbors, or people groups on the other side of the world!

# Prayer
# Missionaries

*What is a prayer missionary?*
*Prayer missionaries are people of any age who*
*pray for lost people, and for those who have*
*been called to reach out to the lost with*
*the Good News of Jesus (missionaries)!*
*Prayer missionaries can be used by God*
*to make a difference in the lives of people*
*around the world through the power of prayer*
*no matter where they live.*

I once heard Esther Ilnisky of the Esther Network International (Children's Global Prayer Movement; see Resources) say that her earliest memories of prayer were crawling around on maps of the world, praying for the lost. "In our family, we have always made it a priority to pray for missionaries, lost people, the nations, and unreached people groups." An unreached people group is a group of people with a similar culture and language who do not have a church that is capable of reaching them for Christ. One tool we used to help us pray was a Missionary Prayer Notebook like the one you will be working on during this journey. It has been a help to us to see the faces of those for whom we pray; however, there are many people that God wants us to pray for whose faces we will never see. He wants everyone to know Him—and without our prayers and the prayers of thousands and even millions of other families, there will be many people who will die without Jesus.

## WHAT YOUR FAMILY WILL DISCOVER ON THIS JOURNEY

> *How to become a prayer missionary by praying for lost people and missionary families right next door and all over the world*

> *How to make a very practical prayer tool to use when you pray for people God loves*

➤ Insights into geography and cultures different from your own

➤ Your family's prayers are encouraging to others

➤ How to have faith and to trust God for His answers to your prayers

📖 MEMORY VERSE:

Psalm 2:8

**STEP ONE** 📖 Practice your memory verse
  ➲ *Collecting materials for a Missionary Prayer Notebook*

📋 MATERIALS NEEDED:

Have the whole family help to collect these materials:

➲ A 3-ring binder (for $8\frac{1}{2}$ x 11 paper)—it's great to have the kind with the clear plastic pocket on the front so you can make a special cover

➲ Pictures and/or prayer cards for missionaries you wish to pray for

➲ Missionary newsletters, e-mails, prayer letters

➲ White or colored paper to fit the binder—you can use colorful acid-free paper if you wish; construction paper is OK but will fade

➲ Notebook paper or other paper with holes punched in

➲ Plastic page protectors

➲ Markers, stickers, maps, newspaper clippings, your own research findings—these can be added as you go

➲ Adhesive—glue sticks are best

➲ Maps—a large map of the world (one that doesn't put the United States in the middle) and a large map of your nation or continent

**Say:** On this journey, we are going to learn how to become prayer missionaries. We will learn some good ways to pray for missionaries and for people who don't know Jesus. When we do this, we'll also pray for different countries and people groups (explain what a people group is using the definition on page 165). To do this, we are going to have to be good detectives!

**Activity:** Find out the names of all the missionaries your family and/or church supports, including the names of the MKs (Missionary Kids)! Also find out where each missionary is serving and what their ministry is: Bible translation, church planting, etc. Get a picture of each missionary/missionary family if you can. If your church doesn't have pictures, you can write to or call each forwarding agent (someone who takes care of a missionary's personal affairs) to request a picture and/or a prayer card. You may have to write to some of the missionaries directly to request their picture. As you request pictures, also ask for prayer requests so that you will know how to pray for the missionaries.

When you have collected some of the pictures (they may not all come at once), you can begin to learn who these missionaries are. Some of you may already know all of your missionaries—that's great! If not, now is a learning time. A parent or older child can tell about each missionary so that your family begins to get familiar with them.

If you have a place where you can put your world map on

the wall, that would be a big help. If not, spread it out on a floor or a table so that everyone can see. Locate the places where the missionaries serve. Tell as much about each family as you can. If your map is on the wall, insert a pushpin into the places where your missionaries serve.

Next, have each member of your family (you will want to pair up young children with an older child or parent) choose at least two missionaries or draw names to match them up. If you have only a few missionaries to choose from, you may only have one apiece. Write down which family member (or team of family members) has which missionaries so there is no confusion later.

**Pray:** Take one missionary family at a time and pray what is on your heart for each one, even though you may not know them very well yet.

**Note:** There are several Side Trips at the end of this journey that will help you to pray effective prayers for missionaries.

**STEP TWO** 📖 Practice your memory verse

➲ *Beginning to make a Missionary Prayer Notebook*

1. Each family member, or family team, needs to gather up materials to make one page of the notebook. For example: one family member will gather a prayer card or picture, colored or construction paper, plastic page protector, a glue stick, markers, newsletters or e-mails from their missionary, etc. You may only have time to make one page today.

2. Find out as much as you can about the people group and nation where your missionaries are located using encyclopedias, atlases, or the Internet. You can put maps, newspaper articles, etc., in your notebook to help you pray! The more you can find out about your missionaries,

the people group(s) they serve, and the country in which they live, the better informed you will be as you pray for them.

3. Once all the materials are collected, begin putting your page together.

> A. Attach pictures of the missionary family and/or their prayer card to your page. On the same side of your picture page, leave room for a map, so you can identify the place where your missionaries live.

> B. Write the missionary's name along with the nation, people group, mission, or any other identifying name you wish somewhere on the page. Be sure to put the names of their children and identify them on the picture. (In our family notebook, we slip e-mails and newsletters into the page protector on the opposite side of the paper with the pictures and maps.)

> C. As each family member or family team finishes their page, slip it into a page protector and place it into the binder.

> D. Now you are ready to pray daily! Stop and take time to pray for each missionary or mission that your family has learned about today. Use the suggestions from the Side Trips section if you wish.

**STEP THREE**  📖 Say your memory verse
➲ *Making a cover page for your Missionary Prayer Notebook*

**Activity:** Make additional pages for the Missionary Prayer Notebook and pray for the new missionaries you have added.
**Read:** Matthew 9:37–38 and discuss what it means.

**Activity:** Use this passage of Scripture to make a cover page for your notebook. You can type it on the computer or do it by hand. Have each member of the family help to decorate the front cover! If you don't have the kind of binder with the plastic slipcover on the front, make a cover page as the first page of your notebook.

**Pray:** Pray that the Lord of the harvest will send more workers into His harvest field. And remember, it might be that God will use someone in your own family (or even ALL of you) to be the answer to your own prayers.

## STEP FOUR  📖 Say your memory verse
➲ *Adding pages to your Missionary Prayer Notebook*

**Pray:** As a family, turn the pages of your completed (or in process) notebook and pray for each missionary family one at a time. Try using the Five Blessings listed in a Side Trip at the end of this journey.

**Watch:** Always be on the lookout for any information in the newspaper, in magazines, or on TV (you'll have to take notes) about the countries and cities where your missionaries live so that you can include this information in your notebook.

## STEP FIVE  📖 Say your memory verse
➲ *Making prayer pages for missionary families*

**Finish:** If you still need to work on your pages, spend some time doing so.

**Pray:** As a family, turn the pages of your notebook and pray for each missionary family.

**Activity:** Make a Prayer Page for each missionary family to help you keep track of the work of God! Be sure to ask missionaries for answered prayer stories! Use the notebook paper or other paper that has holes punched.

**Decide** where your MPN (Missionary Prayer Notebook) will be kept so that everyone can find it and return it to the same place.

**Future:** Now that your MPN is completed, try to remember as a family to use it daily to pray for at least one or two of these families. Keep track of where you leave off each time and continue praying through the notebook until you are ready to start again. Of course, if there is a crisis, illness, etc., in the lives of one of the families, you can certainly make an exception to this order. See some creative ways to use your notebook in the Side Trips section.

## Side Trips

### ➲ Creative ways to use your MPN

Simply by continually reorganizing your notebook from time to time, you can put a fresh perspective on your prayers for missionaries. You can rearrange them

- Alphabetically

- By mission group

- By continent

- Randomly—switch around each time you pray through them all!

- By need—pray first for those who have pressing needs!

Other suggestions:

• Take one page each day and display it in a place where all family members can see it (refrigerator, countertop). Encourage everyone to pray each time they see the picture during the day.

• Take the pages out of the notebook during prayer time so each person has one missionary to pray for. Be sure to return them to the notebook.

• Ask God to show you who needs urgent prayer each day—or be sensitive if one person feels a need to pray for a certain missionary. Perhaps God is prompting you to pray for a special need!

• Get the e-mail addresses of as many of your missionaries and missions as possible. Write and ask them for prayer requests—they will be more than happy to send them! Maybe you could find a family with children around the same ages as yours and become prayer partners with them! Or adopt a single missionary or missionary organization for prayer. Remember to continually ask them to let you know when God answers prayers.

• Keep track of e-mails and newsletters and keep them updated (you may wish to set up some file folders for each missionary to hold older information as you take it out of the notebook to make room for new).

• Write an encouraging e-mail and/or send a card or note or Prayer-A-Gram to the family letting them know that you are praying. Ask to receive their prayer updates if they send them out!

• Assign prayer partners to certain missionaries—for one day or for a whole week. Give daily or weekly reports to the rest of the family on "your" missionary—write for any requests (e-mail or otherwise).

➲ *Biblical prayers for missionaries (A–F)*

Here is a practical, powerful way to pray for your missionaries, taken from the prayer requests of the very first missionary —Paul! (I have adapted the A–F idea developed by T. W. Hunt and Catherine Walker in *Prayer Life: Walking in Fellowship with God*, published by the Sunday School Board of the Southern Baptist Convention.)

**A—Acceptance** (Romans 5:31) —Pray that your missionaries will be accepted by those to whom they minister, as well as by their coworkers and other missionaries serving in the same area.

**B—Boldness** (Ephesians 6:19)—Pray for your missionaries to have courage and boldness in proclaiming the gospel!

**C—Clarity** (Colossians 4:4)—Pray that your missionaries will be clear as they present the gospel—many times in a new language.

**D—Deliverance** (Romans 15:31)—Pray for physical, emotional, and spiritual protection as your missionaries serve.

**E—Extension of ministry** (Colossians 4:3)—Pray for doors to open so that your missionaries can increase their ministry.

**F—Fruitfulness** (2 Thessalonians 3:1)—Pray that the work your missionaries do will bear much fruit and be effective beyond anything they could think or imagine!

### ➲ B–L–E–S–S Your Missionaries

Here is an effective way to pray for missionaries using the Five Blessings, as adapted by missionary friends of mine, Kyle and Kathy Harris. The Harrises minister with Pioneer Bible Translators in Papua New Guinea. Their suggestions on how to pray for missionaries come from personal experience.

### B—Body

Sickness and/or physical harm or the threat of it does more than sap the strength and resources of missionaries. It can lead to discouragement and open them up to further attacks from the Enemy. Sometimes it can even lead missionaries to leave their work.

• For the physical health of missionaries: Psalm 103:2–3; Jeremiah 17:14; and 3 John 1:2

• That they will be protected from harm and kept safe as they travel, speak, teach, translate, etc. Here are some good Scriptures to use as you pray:

1. *For physical strength:* Psalms 28:7; 29:11; 59:9, 16–17; 91; Proverbs 18:10;1 Corinthians 16:13, and Philippians 4:13

2. *For encouragement when missionaries are experiencing a trial or have been through difficult times:* Psalms 31:2; 46:1; 2 Corinthians 12:10; 1 Peter 5:10

### L—Labor

Missionary work, whether it is cross-cultural (done in another culture) or at home, can be very challenging. Schedules can get interrupted, and sometimes progress seems to move along very slowly. The people that missionaries are trying to reach out to with the love of Jesus—to teach or evangelize—are often resistant or even hostile. Remember: families are involved in missionary work in many cases. Parents are often home-schooling children, keeping a household, ministering to the physical needs of those around them as well as to their spiritual needs. Children often help in the work and are busy with school, etc. Here are some Scriptures to help you to pray for the labor of missionaries and their families.

• For encouragement in the face of delays and obstacles and that missionaries will see the opportunities that often come in the midst of these: Psalm 128:2; Proverbs 12:14; 31:17; 1 Corinthians 3:5–9; 15:58; Colossians 3:23; 1 Thessalonians 1:3

• That missionaries will be effective ambassadors of Christ in all they do and say: 1 Thessalonians 5:12–13; 2 Timothy 4:5

• For God to lead as missionaries plan and prioritize: Psalm 90:17

• That missionaries will remember to honor the Sabbath and take time to rest and be refreshed in the Lord: Hebrews 4:10–11

### E—Emotional needs

Missionary work can offer a roller coaster of emotions to individuals and/or families involved in service to the Lord. Successes are often followed by discouraging spiritual attacks. Lack of visible progress, illness, hardships, and loneliness can have a negative impact on the emotional health of missionaries.

• That missionaries would always look to God for their strength in the challenging times: 1 Peter 5:6–7

• For courage and patience: Deuteronomy 1:21; 31:8; Joshua 1:9; Colossians 1:10–12

• That God would do something today that would be an encouragement for missionaries: John 16:33; Ephesians 3:14–19; Philippians 1:6

### S—Social needs

Relationships are the key to your missionaries' effectiveness. Not only do they need to develop strong relationships with the people to whom God has led them to minister, but they also need good relationships with their fellow missionaries. Most importantly, missionaries can get so busy and caught up in ministry that they neglect their most important earthly relationships with their spouse and children.

• That married missionaries will pray together as husband and wife and keep their family spiritually strong and unified, raising their children to honor the Lord: Matthew 18:19–20; Deuteronomy 11:18–19; Psalm 34:11

• That missionaries will develop strong friendships with those they work with and with those to whom they minister: Psalm 133:1; Proverbs 22:11; Ecclesiastes 4:9–10; Romans 15:5–6; Ephesians 4:3

### S—Spiritual needs

Pray for the spiritual needs of missionaries—that they might stay strong in their faith and that their personal lives might be holy and pure. The spiritual battle missionaries face is often greater than they have been prepared to face.

• That they will continually maintain a close, intimate walk with Jesus: Psalm 27:4; Philippians 3:7–11

• That they will put on the armor of God daily: Ephesians 6:10–18

• For spiritual strength day to day and in the midst of whatever spiritual crisis might face them: Psalms 18:32; 27:14; 31:24; 91:11–12; 105:4; 118:14; 147:3; 1 Corinthians 1:8–9; 1 Timothy 1:12

Your prayers can help missionaries who might otherwise become discouraged and come home to stay on the field. Your prayers can help missionaries to be more effective in their work and service. Your prayers can literally be the difference between life and death for those in missionary service.

### ➲ Prayer pennies

Every penny (or nickel or dime) represents a prayer—whenever you pray for a missionary put a penny (or nickel or dime) in the container. When you collect a certain amount, decide on something to purchase and send it to one of your missionary families. Be sure to let them know how you collected the money.

### ➲ Prayer-and-praise piggies

Most of us have used a piggy bank to put money into at one time or another. How about using one to put prayers into? Actually, you will need two banks: One will be the "Prayer Piggy" and the other will be the "Praise Piggy." You can use any kind, but be sure that they are large enough to put your prayer requests into.

Whenever a missionary asks you to pray about something, write it down in your Journey Journal or your Missionary Prayer Notebook. Then make a copy of the prayer request on another small piece of paper, leaving room to write what God does. Pray together over this request. Roll it up and tie it with a small piece of yarn (in a bow, so it's easy to untie). Drop it into the "Prayer Piggy."

At the end of each month, open the bank and let all of the rolled up requests come out. Take turns reading them out loud one by one. Ask, "Has God answered this request?" If so, how has He answered it? Give praise to God for each answer to prayer (even if it wasn't answered the way you prayed or expected) and write it down on the paper. If the request is still unanswered (as far as you know) or if it is very new—set is aside. After you have given God praise for answered prayer, take the praise pile of requests, tie them back up, and put them into the Praise Piggy.

Pick up each paper that is left. Pray earnestly over the new requests and the unanswered requests. Put them back into the Prayer Piggy. Remember, as you put the new ones in, write them in your Journey Journals too (or in your prayer notebook). Talk about the prayers God has answered in a way you didn't expect (maybe someone died and you prayed for them to recover)—and pray that the Lord will be glorified and honored through the unexpected. Perhaps He will generate new prayer requests as a result of this unexpected answer—maybe you need to be praying for the family now or for the work left undone. Perhaps God wants to do something in someone's life and needs you to be praying in a way you didn't expect.

⅄

## HOW TO MAKE THIS
## A JOURNEY FOR A LIFETIME

1. Help to recruit others in your church to pray for missionaries.

2. When missionaries come to visit your church, offer to have them stay in your home.

3. Have children be prayer pen pals with missionary children—on e-mail or snail mail.

4. Make other prayer notebooks for

friends                            school
extended family                    church family
pastors and their families         government officials
police                             firefighters

Make one also for your own family—so that you can all continually lift up one another's needs.

5. Share your notebooks and ideas with others—offer to teach others how to make the notebooks at your church.

6. Continue to find creative ways to pray but don't forget to keep track of answered prayer—it will greatly increase your faith!

# Putting Feet to Your Prayers (Prayerwalking)

*Go, walk through the length and breadth*
*of the land, for I am giving it to you.*

GENESIS 13:17

✷

*Prayerwalking is praying on-site with insight.*

STEVE HAWTHORNE AND GRAHAM KENDRICK,
Authors of *Prayerwalking*

One of the most fun prayerwalks I have ever taken was when my son and I joined the Children's Prayer Congress on a prayerwalk around the White House. You can't walk all the way around the most famous house in America anymore, as the security has been tightened significantly around it. However, in 2001 it was still possible, and some one hundred children of all ages and their sponsors stopped at different stations around the perimeter of the grounds. We prayed for each branch of government and through different sections of the president's inaugural address. It was powerful to hear so many young children lifting their voices in prayer for this nation.

Prayerwalking is, very simply, exactly what its name implies: praying while walking. It is a unique way to pray for neighbors, neighborhoods, schools, and government. Pray as you walk by or near people. Example: You want to pray for your neighbors. As a family, go on a prayerwalk around your neighborhood. Pray quietly for each home and its inhabitants. Don't call attention to yourselves and keep your eyes open as you walk (basic safety precaution). That's all there is to it!

**Note:** The steps for this Journey were adapted from *Seek God for the City,* by Steve Hawthorne, who has also co-authored the book *Prayerwalking* with Graham Kendrick (See Resources).

# WHAT YOUR FAMILY WILL DISCOVER ON THIS JOURNEY

➤ *How to put feet to your prayers as you literally take prayer field trips to pray "on-site with insight"*

➤ *How to pray in creative ways for people, places, and situations in your community*

➤ *How to pray more specifically for people in your city or town as you pray in, on, or through their environment*

 MEMORY VERSE:

*Genesis 13:17*

**STEP ONE** 📖 Practice your memory verse

➲ *Prayerwalk your neighborhood*

**Read:** Romans 15:2; Galatians 5:14

**Walk** around your neighborhood asking the Lord to reveal to you which families need a special touch from Jesus. Remember: God may choose to use you to be the answer to your own prayers.

**Pray** that the Lord will prepare hearts to hear and to receive. Pray for God's peace to be upon the people and/or families who live on your street or in your apartment complex. Ask for the Lord's blessing to rest upon their lives, their relationships with one another, their health, their work, and/or school.

**Be prepared:** Always be ready to give an answer if anyone asks what you are doing: Example: "We're walking through these neighborhoods praying God's blessing on people. Is there any way we can pray for you?"

See Journey #1 to pray the Five Blessings for your neighbors! These are powerful prayers based on the word *bless*. The Five Blessings will give you some specific, focused prayers to pray. Prayerwalking is a great way to be a Lighthouse of Prayer for your neighborhood.

**STEP TWO**  📖 Say your memory verse
➲ *Prayerwalk your school and the schools in your city*

**Read:** Luke 6:40
**Pray:**
• That teachers, administrators, and students will have the opportunity to know Jesus Christ

• That the believers who work in the schools will be diligent about praying for the students and staff who work around them

• That the students who follow Christ will be godly examples to their classmates and teachers according to 1 Timothy 4:12: "Don't let anyone look down on you because you are young, but set an example for the believers in speech, in life, in love, in faith and in purity"

• That the school facilities will be adequate to prepare students and that the curriculum will be pleasing to the Lord; that anything not pleasing to Him will be removed

**STEP THREE**  📖 Say your memory verse
➲ *Prayerwalk city hall, the courthouse, or other government buildings*

**Read:** 1 Timothy 2:1–2

**Pray** quietly on or near the site that best represents the government of your city.

- That city officials will be an example of righteousness

- That these officials will have wisdom and discernment to govern diligently

- That these officials will do nothing to hinder the work of the Lord

- That these officials will come to know Christ and that the center of city government will honor the Lord

If possible, leave a short note for your mayor or another government official that describes your prayers of blessing for him (or her) and for the city (village, town).

## STEP FOUR 📖 Say your memory verse

➲ *Prayerwalk newspaper offices and TV and radio stations*

**Read:** Proverbs 4:24–26
**Pray:**

- That each person will have a personal relationship with Christ and that his position will reflect Christ

- That each person will be truthful in his work and that his reporting will be honest

- That stories glorifying the Lord will be put into print, on television, or on the radio

## STEP FIVE 📖 Say your memory verse

➲ *Prayerwalk nursing homes, hospitals, and other health-care facilities*

**Read:** Psalm 41:1

**Pray** on or near the grounds of a hospital or clinic. If you wish and if it is allowed, you can walk quietly through the halls and pray at a hospital or nursing home facility.

**Pray:**

• That God will protect and strengthen those who are ill

• That God will give kind, loving, and patient servants' hearts to those who work with the ill or elderly

• That those who live there will be encouraged by visits from family and friends

• That the Lord's presence will be evident

## STEP SIX  📖 Say your memory verse

➲ *Prayerwalk police stations and fire stations*

**Read:** Psalm 106:3

**Pray** outside the nearest police or fire station. Leave a personal note to the chief of police (or fire chief) or to someone you know who works on the force, letting him know that Christians are praying for them.

• That they will have wisdom and discernment in their day-to-day work and routines

• That they will experience health and safety

• That their families will experience strength and peace

• That they will be used of God to resist the evil intentions of the Enemy

• That their hearts will be open to know Christ

## STEP SEVEN  📖 Say your memory verse
➲ *Prayerwalk jails and prisons*

**Pray** near a jail, a prison, or a correctional facility. Or, pray near the homes of people who have a family member in prison.

**Read:** Matthew 25:36

**Pray:**

• That each person in prison will have the opportunity to hear the gospel of Jesus Christ

• That the prisons and jails will become places of fellowship in Christ

• That prisoners will be protected from the evil influences of the Enemy

• That prison workers and officials will have compassionate, nonjudgmental hearts

• That the families of prisoners will be protected and will sense the peace of Christ

• That released prisoners will find strength and wisdom to live lives that have been renewed and restored in Christ

## STEP EIGHT  📖 Say your memory verse
➲ *Prayerwalk recruiting offices and/or a military base*

**Read:** Matthew 8:5–10

**Pray** near a military base or recruiting office

• Pray for protection and safety for those in the service of the nation

• Pray for families who have experienced changes due to frequent moving and separation

• Pray for the Lord's light to break through with His gospel of peace

• Pray for chaplains and others who are in positions of spiritual leadership

**STEP NINE**   📖 Say your memory verse

➲ *Drive-by prayer*

**Read:** Galatians 5:19–21

**Pray** for those in high crime areas, adult bookstores, palm-reading parlors, drug houses, X-rated movie theaters, and streets with prostitutes.

Don't put your family in danger when you do this. Terry Teykl tells a wonderful story about two elderly ladies who wanted to prayerwalk in a dangerous neighborhood where rival gangs were very active. They decided to drive instead. As they drove night after night, they prayed earnestly for the gang members. You can read the whole story in Terry's book *Pray and Grow: Evangelism Prayer Ministries* (Nashville: Discipleship Resources, 1988). To make a long story short, the two rival gang members came to Christ. On the day one of the boys baptized the other, they gave a testimony to say that two drive-by shooters were won to the Lord because of the prayers of two drive-by pray-ers.

Sometimes, when the weather is bad or when a neighborhood isn't safe to walk in or when someone in your family is not physically able to walk, drive-by praying is a great idea—besides being practical. It also helps you to cover more ground in a shorter period of time, especially if you want to go to pray at several different places in the community.

**Pray** for places of darkness:

• That those who would choose to establish such businesses and those who would choose to patronize them would have their hearts filled with sorrow and regret and be strongly convicted of their sin

• That Christians will love the sinners but hate the sin—enough to pray in great numbers for the salvation of those who have given themselves to darkness

• That each person who runs such a business will come face-to-face with Jesus and turn his or her heart to Him

• That those buildings now used for the Enemy's work will be transformed and utilized for God-honoring activities or be closed

**STEP TEN**  📖 Say your memory verse

➲ *Prayerwalk churches—your own and others in your community*

**Read:** John 17:21

**Pray:**

• For unity in the body of Christ

• That the community would see pastors praying together and working together

• That God would heal any divisions that separate congregations and pastors from loving one another

• That many would come to Christ as a result of seeing the church in your city coming together in love

# 🌲 Side Trips

➲ *Alternate prayerwalks*

• Make a list of alternate places where your family can prayerwalk—college campuses, local businesses, malls, tourist sites, poorer areas of town, the perimeter of your city or county.

• Prayerwalk your Zip Code. For more information, see Resources.

• Participate in "Seek God for the City," which also includes PrayUSA! and PrayWORLD! Join millions of other Christians all over the world in an annual, forty-day prayer effort asking God to bring about a great spiritual awakening that will transform our cities and our world! See the Resource section for more information.

• Organize prayerwalks for your church. Target the neighborhoods around your church for prayer. You might want to return afterwards with Jesus videos and popcorn as an outreach.

➲ *Prayerwalking is one great way for your family to be a Lighthouse of Prayer in your neighborhood and city. See Journey #1 for more information on Lighthouses.*

## HOW TO MAKE THIS A JOURNEY FOR A LIFETIME

1. Make prayerwalking a regular activity that you and/or your family will choose to do throughout your lives.

How fun to watch prayerwalking pass from one generation to the next—and how powerful!

2. Teach other families to prayerwalk. Invite others to join you to prayerwalk your neighborhoods, local schools, and media (newspaper offices, TV and radio stations). Find some passages of Scripture or use prayers from books such as the Prayers that Avail Much series or the Prayers that Prevail series to help get the pray-ers going. Show them the video *Prayerwalking for Kids* (a snappy, upbeat six-minute video for kids on how to pray for your community). This video can be ordered by going to www.reignbridge.org or by writing or calling Joey and Fawn Parish, 540 W. Highland Drive, Camarillo, CA 93010; 805-987-0064.

3. Always be looking for places that need to be prayerwalked. Perhaps you will read something in the paper about an area in your community where there has been some vandalism, or you may come across several adult bookstores or see a sign on a home that offers palm reading or tarot cards. These may be future sights for prayerwalking. Keep a log or journal of places or areas that could use a touch from God through the prayers of faithful prayerwalkers or drive-by pray-ers.

PART 4

# SPECIAL
# TYPES
# OF PRAYER

# Prayer
# Parties

*This is the day the LORD has made;*
*let us rejoice and be glad in it.*

PSALM 118:24

When my new friend Jan told me about Prayer Parties she had organized at her church and in her home, I got so excited to know more that I begged her to e-mail me all of her ideas. I am so thankful that she has graciously consented to allow me to share some of her ideas, which then inspired and helped me to generate many ideas of my own. The first Prayer Party I held was at a church in Colorado Springs. It was only an hour long, which wasn't nearly enough time! Parents and children came together to learn about prayer in a fun, experiential way and left excited about how easy it would be to do some of these activities as a family at home. So many people think of prayer as a boring activity. Prayer Parties show people that prayer is the divine activity that God has called us to—and it's *fun!*

This journey will help you to plan for and have a Prayer Party of your own. After you throw the first Prayer Party, you will want to have another one . . . and who knows how many others will want to do the same!

## WHAT YOUR FAMILY WILL DISCOVER ON THIS JOURNEY

➤ *Prayer is fun*

➤ *Prayer is exciting, living, and active*

➤ *Prayer is something families can enjoy doing together*

## 🕐 HOW TO PREPARE:

First, try this as a family. Then, invite one or two more families to join you. Involve the whole family in preparation. Decide which games you will do and how long your party will last. (Suggested time with families: sixty to ninety minutes.) Start out with a smaller group (eight to ten). If you have space, you can add more people for the next party. Or you might have a Prayer Party once a month, or once a quarter, and ask different people to host it. You can even begin to stretch the length of your Prayer Parties—even to an all-day or all-night one—as you get more and more excited about it!

Do not serve food during the party. However, when you are finished, you might want to go out for ice cream to celebrate God's goodness and to share your thoughts and feelings about what happened. Or you might want to have a celebration with praise music and pizza. It may also be appropriate to have a Prayer Party without any food at all (Romans 14:17–18).

At the end of each Prayer Party, ask the participants, "What did God do in your life tonight? What new thing about prayer do you know now—or what did God show you?" Who knows —Prayer Parties could catch on like wildfire so that you'll want to try one for your whole church!

## 📖 MEMORY VERSE:

*Psalm 118:24 or 1 Thessalonians 5:16*

**STEP ONE**  📖 Practice your memory verse

 ➲ *Plan your family's Prayer Party!*

**Read:** What is a Prayer Party? Well, it is much like a birthday party or some other kind of celebration—but the guest of honor is God! You can invite small groups or large groups (I suggest starting with a small group—or just begin with your own family). You can invite young people, old people, or in-between people (I suggest that you start out by inviting one or two other families for your first party. Then, blend all different age groups together for more fun and variety). You can have a few prayer activities or lots of them (this will depend on your group).

1. As a family, try out two to five prayer activities listed on pages 199-222. Choose the ones you like the best and begin a list.

2. Start thinking about other families who would enjoy a Prayer Party. Make a list.

3. Decide on a date for your first Prayer Party (with one or two other families) and determine how long the party will be. I suggest that you begin with sixty to ninety minutes. That sounds like a lot of time, but you will wish you had longer!

**Prayer:** Take some time to pray together. Ask the Lord to show you which other families He would like you to invite and pray that He will be honored and glorified by all of your preparations.

## STEP TWO   📖 Say your memory verse

1. Try out two to five more activities. Continue to put the ones you enjoy the most on your list. (Remember—you will only have about sixty minutes. You may wish to keep some on a backup list, in case you have time for them.)

You might want to choose several shorter activities for this first party.

2. Look at the sample Prayer Party invitation below. You may use this or make one of your own. Let everyone help! Decorate them so that they are very personal.

3. Decide which families to invite. (You may wish to have some alternates in case one or more families can't come.)

**Pray:** Pray together that God will stir the hearts of those families you have decided to invite . . . and work out their schedules to be able to attend.

Sample Prayer Party Invitation:

---

### YOU'RE INVITED
### *to a*
### PRAYER PARTY!

**Hosted by:**
**Date:**
**Place:**
**Time:**
**What to Bring:** *Your whole family and your Bibles*

*What's a Prayer Party? It is an opportunity to bring your entire family to a fun-filled hour of exciting prayer. There will be games, crafts, and music! Learn a few new things to do in prayer that you can take home with you. You may even want to have a Prayer Party of your own!*

**RSVP:**

---

(The RSVP is very important! You will need to know who is coming for sure so that you can plan in terms of having enough material! If a family can't come, be ready to invite another.)

**STEP THREE**  📖 Say your memory verse

1. Try out two to five more activities. Continue with your list.

2. Choose the date of your Prayer Party and continue to make your invitations.

3. Choose one member of your family to keep the party going—the "Master of Ceremonies." This person will introduce and explain the games and make sure things move along so that all the activities can be accomplished. If you wish, you can assign different family members to each prayer activity. Everyone gets a chance to explain an activity this way.

**Pray:** Pray that each game or prayer activity you choose will teach your family and the others who attend something new about prayer. Pray that the focus of your prayers during the Prayer Party will line up with the perfect will of God.

**STEP FOUR**  📖 Say your memory verse

1. Try out two to five more activities. How's your list coming?

2. Finish your invitations, if necessary.

3. Make a list of the items you will need to make or collect for the activities you have chosen.

**Pray:** Pray that your family will grow closer together as you plan the Prayer Party. Pray that the Lord will knit you together in love and unity.

## STEP FIVE 📖 Say your memory verse

1. Finish sampling activities today during this step—there will be more opportunities to try the ones you have not gotten to yet. Or there may be several that would be simple to do without a "practice run."

2. Make the final decision on what activities you will have at your first (and hopefully not last) Prayer Party. Make sure there are activities that will appeal to many ages (from youngest to oldest).

3. Using the list you have already made and adding the items needed for activities you have already tried, come up with everything you will need to make or collect before the party.

4. Decide when to mail or deliver your invitations. Be sure to do this several days ahead—a week to ten days is a good amount of time.

**Pray:** Praise the Lord for the opportunity to communicate with Him through prayer. Give Him thanks that you live in a nation where you can freely express your love for Him with your friends and family.

## STEP SIX 📖 Say your memory verse

Consider purchasing or making some small prizes for certain games—be sure they are prayer related. Work through these during this step.

**STEP SEVEN**  📖 Say your memory verse

1. Continue planning and getting ready by having all materials available, deciding who will be in charge of what activity and who will keep score when necessary.

2. Make contact with the families to whom you have sent invitations to make sure they were received. Invite them personally and assure them that they will have a wonderful experience. Let them know that they will not be "called on" or put on the spot to pray out loud. (Some people are very afraid of this.)

3. If you are making prizes, continue working on them.

4. Make sure you are well prepared on the day of your party. If everyone has a good prayer experience, they will want to do it again!

5. Don't forget to pray during each step of the journey!

## PRAYER ACTIVITIES AND GAMES

Please consider the ages of your participants. Pair young children up with older children or adults, so they can take an active part. Be sure you make it clear that everyone will be able to pray at his or her level of comfort. Some people are more comfortable praying silently than out loud. Just encourage everyone to pray in agreement together.

Use any combination of these activities or make up activities of your own. If you come up with some originals, please send them to me!

### ➲ *1. Bible prayer trivia*

## 🕐 TIME NEEDED:

Approximately 15–20 minutes

## 📋 MATERIALS NEEDED:

➲ Bibles

➲ 2 dingers, bells, or buzzers (optional)

➲ 10–20 prepared quiz questions (see below for samples)

Find prayers and people who prayed in the Bible. Make up twenty questions such as the three examples listed after the directions. Divide into two teams prior to the party to save time (mix up people from different families and of different ages—try to make the teams as balanced as possible). Have a scorekeeper and a question reader (with a silly name like Pat Prayerjak or Eugene O'Kneel).

Remember to disqualify members who had anything to do with writing the questions. One point is given for each question answered correctly. Two points are given if the bonus is answered correctly. If a question is answered incorrectly, the other team will get a chance to answer. The team with the most points at the end of the twenty questions wins! You must move as quickly as possible to have time for other games!

Have dingers or buzzers—or just take turns! Make sure that you have Bibles handy in case there is a question. On the answer sheet, make sure you have put down the correct reference. If no one answers the question correctly, go to the verse(s) and share the information so everyone can learn.

**Examples:**

1. Who prayed this prayer? "And she made a vow, saying, 'O LORD Almighty, if you will only look upon your servant's misery and remember me, and not forget your servant but give her a son, then I will give him to the LORD for all the days of his life, and no razor will ever be used on his head'" (1 Samuel 1:11).

**Answer:** Hannah

**Bonus:** What was the name of her son?

**Answer:** Samuel

2. Who often went to lonely places to pray? (See Luke 5:16)

**Answer:** Jesus

**Bonus:** What was one place Jesus went to pray?

**Answer:** A mountainside, a solitary place, Gethsemane

3. Who prayed three times a day facing Jerusalem? (See Daniel 6:10)

**Answer:** Daniel

**Bonus:** Where did Daniel find himself because he continued to pray despite an edict (order) of the king that said he couldn't?

**Answer:** Lion's den

## ➲ 2. Fill-in-the-blank prayer

🕐 TIME NEEDED:

About 5 minutes

📋 MATERIALS NEEDED:

➲ Paper and pencils

This can be done simply or in a more complicated form, depending on the people participating. Have older children or adults pair up with younger children. Give everyone a piece of paper with one or two fill-in-the-blank sentences or phrases on it. Have everyone do the same thing. For example:

Lord, You are _____.

We love You because _____.

Instruct everyone to fill in the blank(s). Then, have everyone stand and take turns reading (or proclaiming) what they have written.

## ➲ 3. The lost coin

🕐 TIME NEEDED:

Approximately 5–10 minutes

📋 MATERIALS NEEDED:

➲ Coins or stamps from several different nations (enough for each person at the party to have a different one). You may wish to put these in small Ziplock bags to keep them from getting damaged.

➲ A map of the world or a globe

Hide the coins or stamps around the room in easy-to-find places (you should do this before the party begins). When you find a coin or a stamp, locate the nation it represents on the map. Next, pray for that nation to turn its heart to Christ. Pray for the people to hear about Jesus and accept Him as Lord and Savior.

Make sure everyone finds a coin within the first couple of minutes so that they will have a few minutes to pray. Give help when needed. When the time is up, say, "'Ask of me, and I will make the nations your inheritance, the ends of the earth your possession' (Psalm 2:8). Lord Jesus, we are asking You for these nations! Draw them to Yourself! In Jesus' name we pray, Amen."

### ➲ 4. Scavenger prayer hunt

 TIME NEEDED:

60 minutes or more (this can be a party all by itself!)

**Suggestion:**
• Be sure to use or adapt the activities for younger children if they are on your team. It's important to give them an opportunity to participate fully in the team effort.

## ▤ MATERIALS NEEDED:

➲ Telephone (cell phones can be used)—all teams need to have equal access. This means that if there is only one telephone available, it is for everyone's use—first come, first served! However, the best scenario is for each team to have a cell phone. Only local calls should be made! If you are in a car, the driver may not use the cell phone.

➲ Bibles

➲ Various maps of the world, an atlas, and/or encyclopedias

➲ *Operation World* (see Resources)

➲ A computer with Internet and e-mail capabilities

➲ If you want to have a prize or prizes for the winning team, you will need to get them ahead of time. Prizes are not necessary, however.

### Directions:

Divide into teams of three or four. Choose one person on each team to be the "scribe." The scribe will keep track of each requirement completed and the points awarded. The first team to finish is the winner. Choose activities from the list below or make up your own. Determine how much time will be given to complete as many requirements as possible.

Ahead of time, assign a point value to each "requirement," keeping in mind that some are more difficult than others. The team that has the most points by the time deadline will be the winner. This activity can be very time consuming, so judge accordingly as you plan your party. One person from your family should be the "official" who is available to answer questions. This person obviously cannot be part of a team and must remain totally neutral.

You need to be sure that all of the teams return to the base (located wherever the official is) at the designated time for the scavenger hunt to end. Any team that is not present at that time will be assessed a five-point penalty for every minute they arrive late (or whatever penalty you wish to assess).

1. A timer or second hand on a watch will be needed. Designate one person to be the timekeeper. Each team member needs to draw a picture of his or her most recent answer to prayer or act it out. One at a time, take turns showing your picture of acting out your answer to prayer for your teammates. They must guess your answer to prayer within one minute. Your team will get one point for each correct response up to five points. Have the scribe write down each person's name and their answered prayer, even if it was not guessed within the time limit. When everyone has had a turn, give God praise for answered prayer. **Point Value: 5**

2. Find one prayer in the Bible and list the Scripture, who the pray-er was, and how God responded to the prayer. **Point Value: 2**

3. Each member of the team will call a non-Christian friend or relative and ask for one prayer need. Write down the person's name and prayer request. Stop and pray for this person as a group. **Point Value: 3**

4. Ask one neighbor in one neighborhood represented by your team for a prayer need. Write down the person's name and prayer need. **Point Value: 3**

5. Visit a pastor or staff person from a team member's church and get at least one written prayer request. Have

the pastor sign the paper. Then pray for the pastor or staff person before you leave. **Point Value: 6**

6. Choose one nation with the initial of the first name of your youngest team member. Write down (1) their primary language, (2) their primary religion, and (3) one other major fact about the nation that would affect their openness to Jesus Christ. Together, pray that the Lord will draw the people in this nation to Himself! **Point Value: 7**

7. Get one recent and still relevant prayer request from one of the missionaries your church supports. Hint: You can use e-mail or phone someone on the missions team. Pray as a team for this missionary and family. **Point Value: 4**

8. Ask one other family member or person at the Prayer Party for a prayer request. This person must be on a different team. Write it down and have the person sign the paper. Pray together for this person's request. **Point Value: 3**

9. Have each team member write down three prayer requests. Be sure each person's name is above each set of requests. Get in a circle. Pray for the person on your right as you go around the circle. **Point Value: 3**

10. Make up some of your own activities if you wish to! Be creative!

When this activity is finished, add up the points (don't forget to subtract the "late" points) and declare a winner. Next, get into your teams and pray once again (chances are you didn't take a lot of time to pray during the activity phase of the prayer hunt, so now is your chance to focus on the prayer requests you have been given). For example, pray prayers of thanksgiving for the answered prayers, pray for the prayer requests you have gathered, pray for the nation you chose, and pray for the missionary prayer requests.

To close the prayer time, play or sing a lively worship song (two good ones are "Shine, Jesus, Shine" and "Celebrate, Jesus, Celebrate").

### ➲ 5. Missionary prayers

🕐 TIME NEEDED:

15 minutes

📑 MATERIALS NEEDED:

➲ 5 x 8 index cards with the names of the missionaries and mission outreaches your church supports written on the top

➲ Pictures or prayer cards (if available)

➲ An atlas, maps, the book *Operation World*, encyclopedias, and other resources you think would be helpful

➲ Recent newsletters and/or e-mails from the missionaries

Divide into family teams, depending on how many people are at the Prayer Party. Draw the name of one missionary family —find out as much about them as you can in a short period of time (ten minutes). Locate their nation or location on a map (even if they are located in the United States). Write on the card three prayer requests for them, three for the people they minister to, and three for the country in which they work based on your research (remember to look at e-mails and newsletters—

you might get exactly what you need). Take five minutes to pray for these needs and requests.

### ➲ 6. Yarn maze

🕐 TIME NEEDED:

5–10 minutes

▤ MATERIALS NEEDED:

➲ Yarn or ribbon

➲ 3 x 5 cards with prayer requests written on them

Put together several simple trails of yarn or ribbon for people to untangle. It's best to do this out-of-doors or in a large indoor area away from the other scheduled activities, so it can be prepared ahead of time. Have enough "trails" depending upon how many people are present. They can work individually or as teams. It is most fun when they have to interact with one another when they get briefly tangled up. Each person or team needs to untangle the yarn and follow it to a prayer need at the end. Instruct them to pray for the need expressed.

**Suggestion:**
Make specific requests for your pastor and your church; the president of the United States and his advisors, staff, and family; missionaries, etc. Put these requests on 3 x 5 cards. Example: "Pray for the safety of our youth pastor and his wife as they travel to a conference this weekend."

## ⮑ 7. *Household prayer*

🕐 TIME NEEDED:

5–10 minutes

📰 MATERIALS SUGGESTED:

⮑ Large basket

⮑ Household items, such as: telephone, scissors, Band-Aid, towel, toothbrush, floss, veggie peeler, book, comb, safety pin, potholder, hanger, coffee cup, mirror, envelope, hairbrush, newspaper

Bring out a basket with lots of common household things in it. Have each person reach in and take one! Instruct them to thank God for something in their lives that it represents. Be creative.

**An envelope:** "Thank You, Lord, for enveloping me with Your love."

**A safety pin:** "Thanks, Lord, for holding me together during tough times."

**A Band-Aid:** "Thanks for being our Healer."

Share with the prayer partiers that lasting effects will take place with this activity if they will give themselves visual reminders of how to pray without ceasing around their homes by attaching prayer reminders to common household items!

An example of a prayer reminder (or prayer trigger): My husband has trained himself to pray as soon as the hot water from the shower hits him. Why? Because when he went to camp one year, the water was *cold!* He was so thankful for hot water when he got home that he decided never to take it for granted again. So, he often begins his prayer time in the shower by giving praise to the Lord for wonderful, hot water.

You can train yourself (along with others in your family) how to use prayer reminders or triggers each day! You might have many of them! Yours might not be the hot water, but it might be your nice, soft pillow, reminding you to pray before going to sleep. Train yourself that every time your head hits that pillow, it's time to pray. You can even use the household items introduced in this game. Train yourself to pray whenever you use one of these items. Pretty soon, your whole day will be filled with prayer and praises to the Lord!

### ➲ 8. Popcorn prayer

### 🕐 TIME NEEDED:

5–10 minutes

### 📋 MATERIALS NEEDED:

➲ Beanbag filled with unpopped popcorn, if possible

Toss a beanbag or an actual bag filled with unpopped popcorn around the room, giving praises to God, praying for someone, or lifting up thanks to Him whenever you catch the bag! Move quickly so that His name is lifted up continually during the time. Explain that we can pray at all times, even if we just lift up some really short, quick prayers during the day. People can think of these prayers as "popcorn" prayers using the visual image of popcorn popping. Examples:

• Lord, thank You for our pastor.

• Father, we praise You for the beautiful rainbow we saw this afternoon!

• Awesome God, help us to give You glory in everything we do and say!

### ➲ 9. Penny prayerwalk ("Praying on-site with insight")

🕐 TIME NEEDED:

20–30 minutes

See Journey #10, "Prayerwalking," for more information.

If it is going to be dark when and where you walk, consider asking everyone to bring a flashlight. Also, this one might be preempted by rain, so have an alternate activity picked out.

Split up into groups of two or three and prayerwalk your neighborhood or around your church. Flip a penny when you begin and at each corner. If it's heads, turn left; if it's tails, turn right. Pray for the homes on both sides of the street as you go. Have one person draw a map of the streets and the route you take. Flip the coin a predetermined number of times (five is a good number) so that you don't get too far away from where you started. Obviously, if the blocks are long, you will want to modify this. If more than one group is headed the same direction, take opposite sides of the street. In the interest of time, you may wish to meet back at your starting point after an agreed-upon time.

## ⊃ 10. Praying by name

### 🕐 TIME NEEDED:

Approximately 10 minutes (depends upon how many people are being prayed for)

When arriving at the party, each person fills out a card with his or her name and three prayer requests on it that they would like the group to pray about. At a certain point in the party, take some time to pray for one another out loud. Put each person in the center, one by one, and lay hands on them!

## ⊃ 11. Paper prayer chain

### 🕐 TIME NEEDED:

10–15 minutes

### 🗐 MATERIALS NEEDED:

⊃ Colorful construction paper cut in strips for a paper chain

⊃ Tape

⊃ Markers or pens

Have everyone write the name of an unsaved friend or family member on as many pieces of paper as there are people at the party. Make a chain to take home, so that all of the names are easy to see on the outside. Make a covenant (agreement) with one another to pray at least once a week over the next month for the people represented by the chain. Hosts give out a list of prayers to pray such as this one:

• Father, I bring the name of _____ before You, because You call us to pray for everyone! (1 Timothy 2:1–6)

• Lord, sometimes it seems like there are some people who will never come to know You. Help us to be faithful, because in You, *all* things are possible. (Mark 10:27)

• Heavenly Father, would You draw _____ to Yourself? (John 6:44)

• Lord, would You please remove the blinders from _____'s eyes so that he/she can see Jesus instead of being deceived by the Enemy? (2 Corinthians 10:3–6)

• Father, we pray in the authority of the name of Jesus that _____ will be known as Your child! (Romans 10:13; Philippians 2:9–11)

• Lord, we thank You for Your victory in overcoming every obstacle that has kept _____ from accepting You as Savior and Lord! (1 Corinthians 15:57)

If someone on the list comes to Christ, notify the host of the party so that the word can be passed along. Otherwise, it is up to you how you wish to pass along that information.

### ⊃ 12. Stick it to the pastor (in prayer)

🕐 TIME NEEDED:

5–10 minutes

## 📋 MATERIALS NEEDED:

- ➲ Sticky notes—have several pads

- ➲ Pens

Everyone write encouraging prayers for your pastor and his family on sticky notes—keeping them intact. The following Sunday, choose a central place to meet and let everyone take the prayer he or she wrote. Then, the whole group can descend upon the pastor with the notes and stick it to him—blessing him with prayer!

**Note:** It's probably a good idea to wait until *after* the service. You can do this for anyone—Sunday school teachers, friends. You can bet that your pastor or friend will be blessed beyond measure! It will be a lifetime memory.

### ➲ 13. Prayers that are caught

## 🕐 TIME NEEDED:

10–15 minutes

## 📋 MATERIALS NEEDED:

- ➲ Any kind of stick (even a 12-inch ruler will do)

- ➲ String

- ➲ A small magnet

- ➲ Paper clips

- ➲ Prayer suggestions written on small pieces of paper

Write down at least one prayer suggestion for each person present. Some suggestions could be:

- Pray for someone who needs Jesus.

- Pray for the children in Afghanistan.

- Pray for the president and his family.

- Pray for the schools in this community.

Attach a paper clip to each paper and drop them into a box. Put the box behind a couch, or the far side of a table, or on the floor. Make a fishing pole with the stick and the string, attaching the magnet to the end. Have each person go fishing for a prayer suggestion. As each one is pulled up, take time to pray together, out loud or silently for each request.

### ➲ 14. Putting all your eggs in one prayer basket

🕐 TIME NEEDED:

10–15 minutes

▤ MATERIALS NEEDED:

➲ Plastic eggs

➲ One basket or container for each team

Write prayers and praises to put into each egg. Have about five eggs for each team. Hide them around a room, or outside, if you wish. Divide into teams of two to four people (remember to put young children with older children or adults who will help them). Instruct the teams to find only five eggs and then wait for other teams to finish. Remember to keep track of where the eggs are hidden, so that they can all be found. When all of the teams have found their five eggs, have them form prayer circles. Take turns reading the notes in the eggs and pray and praise, depending upon what is written on each paper. Give them about five minutes to complete their prayers and praises.

## ➲ 15. Listening prayer

### 🕐 TIME NEEDED:

10 minutes

### 📃 MATERIALS NEEDED:

➲ Prayer journals

➲ Bibles

Give each person a copy of a psalm or direct them to a special passage in their Bibles. Have them read it silently and meditate on it, asking the Lord to help them apply it to their lives. Ask them to wait quietly before the Lord for about five minutes. Have them journal quietly if they wish. Some good passages are:

| | | |
|---|---|---|
| Psalm 1:1–3 | Psalm 18:25–36 | Psalm 37:3–11 |
| Psalm 4:3–4 | Psalm 20:4–5 | Psalm 67 |
| Psalm 8 | Psalm 23 | Psalm 86:11 |
| Psalm 14:2 | Psalm 25:4–5 | Psalm 105:1–4 |
| Psalm 15 | Psalm 27:4 | Psalm 139:23–24 |

## ◌ 16. Pray around the world

🕐 TIME NEEDED:

Approximately 5–10 minutes

📋 MATERIALS NEEDED:

◌ An inflatable plastic globe or a real globe—preferably updated in the past two or three years. Such globes are available from the Caleb Project (see Resource section). Look for plastic beach ball-sized globes at stores like Wal-Mart.

*If you are using a lightweight plastic globe:* Have all of your guests get in a large circle. Toss the ball from one person to another. At each stop, the person who receives the ball is to name a country. Have two or three people pray short sentence prayers for that nation. Then, toss the ball again. Go until each person has had an opportunity to choose a nation.

*If you are using a spinner globe:* Take turns spinning the globe and stopping where your finger lands. Pray in the same manner as above. If you wish, you can have some specific prayer suggestions for each "stop."

## ◌ 17. Pin the prayer on the missionary

🕐 TIME NEEDED:

10 minutes

## 🗐 MATERIALS NEEDED:

⮑ Blindfold

⮑ Box or basket with the names of missionaries and their organizations or countries where they serve written on paper in big, bold lettering

⮑ Pins or pushpins

⮑ A large map of the world (one where the United States is *not* in the center). The map should be one that you don't mind having pins stuck into and should probably be mounted on corkboard or something similar so that it will absorb the pin pricks rather than your wall!

Put up the map of the United States, the world, your state, or your city. Have a box with the names of missionaries in the areas where they serve. Each person in turn will select a name and will immediately be blindfolded. See who can get the closest to the missionary they have chosen. Or have prayers of blessing written on paper (see Journey #12, "The Family Blessing," for blessings to use).

Blindfold each person and pin your blessings onto the map.

In either version, when everyone is finished, pray for the missionaries and also pray blessings on the people and places where your pins are!

⮑ *18. Prayer collage*

## 🕐 TIME NEEDED:

15–20 minutes

# ▤ MATERIALS NEEDED:

⮡ Colorful construction paper

⮡ White poster board

⮡ Magazines and newspapers (with recent events)

⮡ Maps (reproduced to cut up and use)

⮡ Church newsletters or other publications with prayer needs listed

⮡ Pictures of missionaries or church staff (these can be scanned copies)

⮡ Glue sticks, Elmer's glue

⮡ Markers or crayons or colored pencils

⮡ Scissors

⮡ Optional: stickers or other materials to decorate with

**Suggestion:** Ask people to bring some of these materials when they come!

Divide into groups or families. Make a prayer collage out of the magazines and newspapers. When your group is finished, pray over each event or situation represented on your collage. You can lay hands on the pictures as you pray. The advantage to doing this as a family activity is that the collage can be taken home and used as a reminder to pray!

## ⮡ 19. A–Z prayer praises

# ⏱ TIME NEEDED:

10–15 minutes

Depending on how many people are at the party, you may want to break into groups of no more than six or eight. Smaller children can partner with an older child or an adult. Begin with A and say, "Lord, You are _____." Fill in the blank with a word beginning with the letter "A" that describes God. You might say, "Awesome!" The next person says, "Lord, You are awesome and _____ (filling in a word beginning with "B" ). Continue around the circle and through the alphabet.

No one is "out" if they can't remember what comes next—help each other to get all the way around through Z! You might have to stretch things a bit! Here are some examples for each letter that can be used in a pinch:

A — awesome, amazing
B — beautiful, big
C — caring, compassionate
D — divine, delightful
E — excellent, exciting
F — faithful, fun, forever
G — great, good, glorious
H — high above the heavens, huge
I — invisible, invincible
J — just, joyful, Jehovah
K — kind, knowledgeable
L — loving, living
M — majestic, mighty
N — name above all names, nice, near
O — omniscient, over all
P — powerful, patient
Q — quick to forgive
R — righteous, ruler
S — sovereign, strong
T — truth, tremendous

| U | — | understanding, universal |
|---|---|---|
| V | — | virtuous, the vine |
| W | — | wonderful |
| X | — | xcellent, xceptional |
| Y | — | Yahweh |
| Z | — | zealous |

## ➲ 20. Prayer partners

🕑 TIME NEEDED:

About 40 minutes (in three separate sections: 5 minutes, 30 minutes, 5 minutes). This game can be started at the beginning of the party and finished at the end. The 30-minute period is "waiting time" while the "ink" drives.

🗒 MATERIALS NEEDED:

➲ Salt

➲ Water

➲ Pencils

➲ Small paintbrushes (toothpicks could also be used, but paint brushes work best)

Jesus said that if two or more people agree about anything they pray for, God will answer them. Jesus also said that where two or more Christians get together in His name, He is in their midst. A big part of being a Christian is helping other people, and a great way to do that is through prayer.

Choose someone in your family to be your prayer partner. Or you can choose a prayer partner outside of your family.

Each day you can pray for one another. To let each other know what prayers you need, you can trade private notes that are written in invisible ink. Here is a recipe:

> Mix 1 tsp salt and 1 tsp hot water to make the ink. Dip a toothpick or paintbrush in the ink and write your prayer request lightly on a piece of paper. Let the message dry for at least half an hour, then give it to your prayer partner. He or she can make the message reappear by rubbing it with a pencil.

## 🌲 *Side Trips*

### ➲ *Progressive Prayer Party*

Drive to different locations for different games.

### ➲ *Light the night—October 31 each year*

Have a Prayer Party on October 31 in your yard or garage. Invite others to join you as they come by. Give the children and their parents small gifts having to do with prayer. Light the night!

### HOW TO MAKE THIS
### A JOURNEY FOR A LIFETIME

1. Have regular Prayer Parties for your neighborhood—or a block Prayer Party! Invite other families who aren't Christians to come to a Prayer Party. Put them in groups of your Christian friends who will make them feel comfortable. Just have fun! You can prepare them

ahead of time but put their minds at ease that they will not be called upon to pray at any time! But they can be prayed for!

2. Pass along the Prayer Party idea to others!

3. Make this a tradition to pass along through several generations!

# The Family Blessing

*Finally, all of you, live in harmony with one
another; be sympathetic, love as brothers,
be compassionate and humble.
Do not repay evil with evil or insult
with insult, but with blessing,
because to this you were called
so that you may inherit a blessing.*

1 PETER 3:8–9

One of the most meaningful ways to love others is to bless them. You can bless someone by your actions, a meaningful touch or look, or your words. However, one of the best ways to bless someone is to pray blessings into his or her life. Giving scriptural blessings to others in prayer is a powerful way to encourage them. Parents, pray blessings over your children before they go to bed at night. I have prayed Numbers 6:24–26 over my youngest son for years. He is now a teenager, and he still wants to be blessed every night. I know without a doubt that he will bless his own children when he becomes a father.

Blessing your children before a test at school, when they are afraid, or as they are trying to make important decisions is something children cherish and keep in their hearts always. Many scriptural blessings can be prayed just as they are written. Others can be adapted to prayer by changing pronouns or by putting in the name of the person you are blessing. As you lead by blessing your children, they will also learn to bless others—including you! Encourage siblings to bless each other. Make cards with blessings on them for family members, friends, and neighbors. God's Word will not return void. "So is my word that goes out from my mouth: It will not return to me empty, but will accomplish what I desire and achieve the purpose for which I sent it" (Isaiah 55:11).

# WHAT YOUR FAMILY WILL DISCOVER ON THIS JOURNEY

➤ *Special blessings to pray: as a family, for one another, and for others*

➤ *God works through your blessings*

➤ *Praying God's blessings into the lives of others blesses you too*

## ▤ MATERIALS NEEDED:

Read through the daily activities and Side Trips to determine what you will want to have on hand.

➲ Bibles

➲ Concordance (optional)

➲ Journey Journals or paper

➲ Pens, pencils, crayons, and markers

➲ Paper or journals

➲ Note cards and/or Prayer-A-Grams (see Resources)

➲ Three-ring notebook, plastic page protectors, (optional).

## ▥ MEMORY VERSE(S):

*Adults and older children: 1 Peter 3:8–9*
*Younger children: Matthew 5:3–11 (choose one or two verses to memorize)*

**STEP ONE**   📖 Practice your memory verse(s)
➲ *Read: Romans 15:5–6; 2 Thessalonians 3:5; Psalm 65:4*

**Ask:** What is the very best thing God has ever done for you? Share your answers.

➲ *A blessing hunt*

**List** all the blessings God has given you. How has He shared His goodness with you? Write down at least five to ten blessings (little ones can draw pictures of their blessings) and share several with each other, taking turns.

**Pray:** Thank God for the blessings He has given you!

## 🌲 Side Trip

➲ *Blessing reminders*

Put up your written and drawn blessings all around the house as a constant reminder of how good God is! Be creative. Every time you see one of the blessings, written or in picture form, stop to give God thanks for it! Use them as reminders to bless others and to pray for them to receive the blessings God has given you. As you learn different scriptural blessings, write them down and place them around the house as well. Learn as many blessings as you can, so you can continually give them to others. Be creative!

**STEP TWO**   📖 Say your memory verse(s)
➲ *Read: Hebrews 13:20–21*

**Read:** Allow God to bless you through His Word. Choose one of these blessings of encouragement to share with each member of your family today through a picture, a note, or by blessing them face-to-face: 1 Kings 8:57–58; Psalm 20:1, 5; Romans 15:13; 2 Corinthians 13:14; 1 Thessalonians 3:12–13; 2 Thessalonians 2:16–17; 3:5, 16

**Pray together:** Ask the Lord to help you to be a blessing just as He has blessed you.

## ⛏ Side Trip

Who else could you bless today? Your teacher, a coworker, a classmate, the person who delivers your mail? Look for opportunities to bless other people in some way today—through a note, a word of encouragement, an act of kindness, prayer.

**STEP THREE** 📖 Say your memory verse(s)
➲ *Read: 1 Chronicles 16:43*

**Choose** one of these blessings to be your family blessing. Bless one another before you go to bed, before leaving for school, before leaving for work: Numbers 6:24–26; Deuteronomy 28:6; Psalms 20:4; 115:15; 67:1. There are *many* others to choose from. Have someone type out the blessing or put it in some kind of form that you can display in a prominent place in your home. When others ask you about it, you can share with them the blessing of blessing! This is a good way to encourage others to share in this wonderful biblical practice.

**Pray together:** Lord, use us to start a new tradition of blessing others—not just in our own family but in our neighborhood, our church, and throughout our community.

# ♫ Side Trip

➲ *Family blessing*

Write your own blessing as a family. You can use Scripture directly or modify it to fit your family's circumstances. Here is an example: "Lord, bless our family as we wake, as we go through our day, and as we sleep. May You protect us from the Enemy's harmful ways. May we be kept from temptation. Father, we ask that You will bless each thought, each word that comes out of our mouths, and each action we take every day of our lives, so that we will reflect Jesus to others. May we be kept in perfect peace by the knowledge of Your presence in us." When you write your blessing, find a way to frame it and put it in a place where your family can see it often. Each night of this journey, read it out loud together and be blessed!

## STEP FOUR 📖 Say your memory verse(s)

➲ *Starting a Blessing Book*

📋 MATERIALS NEEDED:

➲ Construction paper

➲ Staples

➲ Scissors

➲ Markers, crayons

**Read:** Psalm 90:17

Begin to make a book of blessings as a family. Start collecting these blessings and putting them into categories. What are some categories you can use? How about blessings for sleep, blessings for wisdom, blessings for living godly lives? Then you will have a blessing for every occasion to uplift every member of your family. You may wish to start with the ones you have already learned in previous steps of your journey. Whenever you find new blessings, put them in your book.

**Pray together:** Give God thanks for His awesome Word that is filled with life-giving blessings for everyone! Ask Him to continue to show you the blessings in His Word day by day.

## 🌲 Side Trips

### ⤵ Blessing Books for friends

Make a Blessing Book as a gift for another family. It could be for your pastor's family or for a neighbor or relative. Have everyone participate. On some pages you could list ways people in this family have blessed you: "Thank You, Lord, for my friend Julie, who blesses me by taking time to pray for me when I need her to." On other pages, write prayers of blessing for the family and for individuals in the family.

### ⤵ Birthday blessing party

Make a Blessing Book for the person with the birthday. Have family members and friends write down memories, Scriptures, and godly advice on a paper to be put into a plastic page protector or laminated and placed in the book ahead of time. Invite everyone to come to a birthday blessing celebration. Each person present can read his or her advice and stories to the person being blessed. Then, form a prayer circle around the birthday person, lay hands on him, and pray. I guarantee it will be a birthday that is remembered forever. Thanks to my friends Tom and Debbie Morse, who invited me to their daughter Angela's birthday blessing party on the occasion of her thirteenth birthday. It was certainly a blessing to me, and I have passed the idea on ever since.

### ➲ Blessing parties for other milestones

Give similar parties to bless people on anniversaries, graduations, retirements, and promotions—any special family or friendship occasion.

## STEP FIVE  📖 Say your memory verse(s)

### ➲ A seat of blessings

**Jesus gave us a beautiful example of blessing** (Mark 10:13–16).

Take turns putting one family member after another into the "seat of blessing." Put them in a chair and lay hands on them. Pray for them and give them blessings. Do this when someone is facing a big test the next day, when a family member has had a particularly bad day, or just as an encouragement to build someone up. Be sure to let that person know how special he or she is to you and to God. Examples: "Lord, bless Mary as she studies for her test tonight. Bless her with wisdom and help her to learn all of the material." Or, "Father, bless my mother with the peace that passes all understanding."

## STEP SIX  📖 Say your memory verse(s) each day and continue to encourage one another!

### ➲ Passing on a blessing

**Read:** Genesis 12:3

This Scripture is about Abraham, who was blessed by God to be a blessing. We have been blessed to be a blessing too!

Start looking for ways to bless others as God has blessed you. If He blesses you financially, how can you bless someone else financially? If you were shown mercy, how can you show mercy to someone else? Make it a point never to go to sleep at night without blessing at least one person a day. Try to bless every person in your family at least once a day too. Apply what you have learned about blessings as often as possible! *Pray* blessing on others!

➲ *Additional blessings to share with others*
Psalms 5:12; 29:11; 34:8; 68:3; 84:12; James 1:12; 1 Peter 3:13–14; Jude 1:2

➲ *Blessings for husbands to give to wives*
Proverbs 31:28–31

➲ *Blessings for wives to give to husbands*
Jeremiah 17:7–8

➲ *A good blessing for children to give their parents*
Psalms 112:1–2; 128:6; Isaiah 44:3

➲ *Blessings for parents to give their children*
See the blessings for Step Three; also Psalm 119:1–3; Proverbs 23:25; 1 Thessalonians 5:23; 2 Peter 1:2

➲ *A family blessing*
1 Kings 8:57–58

# 🌲 Side Trips

➲ *Bless this house*

**Read:** Proverbs 24:3–4

**Pray together:** "Father, we pray that our home and family will be built by wisdom and established through understanding. Because of knowledge of Your ways, may the rooms of our home be filled with rare and beautiful treasures so that You will be honored and glorified."

Pray blessings over your home. Walk through each room—anoint doorposts (use olive oil if possible and pray that it will be set apart for God's purposes), read Scripture, praise God, pray scriptural prayers over your home. Set apart (consecrate) your home for the service of the Lord.

If you wish, invite other families to join you. This might even set off a chain reaction of many families dedicating their homes to God. Imagine what He could accomplish in and through the hospitality offered in your home. If you are building a new home, write Scriptures on the walls in pencil before it is painted. (Trust me from personal experience—if you use anything other than pencil, you may have to use more coats of paint than planned.) Pray over every area, dedicating it to God. You will always know that the Word of the Lord is a permanent part of your home.

My friend Pat took the passage from Deuteronomy 6:4–9 and applied verse 9 very literally: "Write them on the doorframes of your houses and on your gates." On the wooden door frame of her side door were written multiple Scripture verses. There was a pencil attached to a string tacked into the door frame, too, so anyone could add a verse or two. It was a blessing to me to stand for a few moments outside reading the Word of the Lord before entering the house.

Here are some good Scriptures to pray over your home, although there are many others you can use as well: Proverbs 24:3–4; Luke 10:5; Acts 10:2. See if you can find additional ones.

## ➲ Blessings for "newness"

Bless new babies and their families, adopted children and their families, new businesses.

## ➲ Family blessing breakfast

Once a month (or more often, if you wish), have a family blessing breakfast. Choose a different person each month to receive special blessing or just take turns blessing one another.

⟩⟨

# HOW TO MAKE THIS
# A JOURNEY FOR A LIFETIME

1. Look for opportunities to pray blessings on others. Make it a daily goal to bless at least one person in some way!

2. Don't forget to pray blessings into the lives of those in your family, as well as friends, coworkers, fellow students, and others.

3. Continue to add to your own blessing book and to make them for others.

 # Conclusion

*This is the confidence we have in approaching
God: that if we ask anything according
to his will, he hears us. And if we know
that he hears us—whatever we ask—
we know that we have what we asked of him.*

1 JOHN 5:14-15

It is my prayer that these journeys have been a blessing to your family and that you have all learned how to draw closer to the Lord in prayer as a result of your experiences. I pray that a flame has been ignited within each of you that will spread to other families in your church, community, nation, and around the world! Prayer is so powerful—and God longs for His people to drink deeply from the well of His boundless resources. As you have learned many new things, don't let yourself be overwhelmed. Let the Lord lead you on the journeys that lie ahead. He will always be faithful to speak to your hearts at just the right moments. He will always answer as you are obedient in asking.

Our gracious Father desires to pour out His blessings and power upon this planet through us—His family upon this earth! May we be careful to stay attached to the Vine through devoted lives of prayer. Remember—communicating with God is not difficult . . . just spend time talking and listening to Him. May your relationships with Jesus grow stronger with each step your family takes in the lifelong journey of prayer.

# Prayer Journey Resources

## BOOKS

Arkins, Anne, and Gary Harrell. *Watchmen on the Walls: Praying Character into Your Child.* Sisters, Oreg.: Multnomah, 1996.

Barnes, Emile, and Bob Barnes. *15 Minute Devotions for Couples.* Eugene, Oreg.: Harvest House, 1995.

Berndt, Jodie. *Praying the Scriptures for Your Children.* Grand Rapids: Zondervan, 2001.

Copeland, Germaine. *Prayers that Avail Much.* 3 vols. Various eds. Tulsa: Harrison House, 1989–2000.

Curtis, Eastman. *Every Day I Pray for My Teenager: A Handbook of Spiritual Prayers for the Mothers of Teenagers.* Lake Mary, Fla.: Creation House; 1997.

Durbin. Kara. *Parenting with Scripture: A Topical Guide for Teachable Moments.* Chicago: Moody, 2001.

Fuller, Cheri. *When Children Pray: How God Uses the Prayers of a Child.* Sisters, Oreg.: Multnomah, 1997, 1998.

————. *When Couples Pray: The Little-Known Secret to Lifelong Happiness in Marriage.* Sisters, Oreg.: Multnomah, 2001.

————. *When Families Pray.* Sisters, Oreg.: Multnomah, 2001.

————. *When Mothers Pray.* Sisters, Oreg.: Multnomah, 1997.

Fuller, Cheri, and Ron Luce, *When Teens Pray.* Sisters, Oreg.: Multnomah, 2002.

Hawthorne, Steve. *Seek God for the City.* Order from Waymakers at www.waymakers.org.

Hawthorne, Steve, and Graham Kendrick. *Prayer-Walking: Praying On-Site with Insight.* Lake Mary, Fla.: Creation House, 993.

Hunt, Art (Arthur). *Praying with the One You Love.* Sisters, Oreg.: Multnomah, 1996.

Johnstone, Jill. *You Can Change the World,* 2 vols. Grand Rapids: Zondervan, 1993.

Johnston, Patrick, and Jason Mandryk. *Operation World: When We Pray God Works.* 6th ed. Waynesboro, Ga.: Authentic Media, 2001.

Kopp, David, and Heather Kopp. *Praying the Bible with Your Family.* Colorado Springs: Waterbrook, 2000.

Linamen, Karen Scalf. *Parent Warrior. Protecting Your Children Through Prayer.* Grand Rapids: Revell, 1999.

Lingo, Susan. *Teaching Our Children to Pray.* Cincinnati: Standard, 1994.

McDowell, Josh; with Bob Hostetler, ed. *Josh McDowell's One Year Book of Youth Devotions.* Wheaton, Ill.: Tyndale, 1999.

Moore, Carey, Pamela Rosewell Moore, and Ruth Bell Graham. *What Happens When Husbands and Wives Pray Together?* Grand Rapids: Revell, 1999.

Nappa, Mike, and Amy Nappa. *52 Fun Family Prayer Adventures.* Minneapolis: Augsburg Fortress, 1996.

Omartian, Stormie., Christopher Omartian, and Amanda Omartian. *The Power of a Praying Parent.* Eugene, Oreg.: Harvest House, 1995.

Osborne, Rick. *Teaching Your Child How to Pray.* Chicago: Moody, 1997.

Pegues, Beverly, and Nancy Huff, eds. *A Call to Prayer for the Children, Teens, and Young Adults of the 10/40 Window.* Seattle: YWAM, 2002.

Rainey, Dennis, and Barbara Rainey, contrib. *Moments Together for Couples.* Ventura, Calif.: Gospel Light, Regal Books, 1995.

Rainey, Dennis, and Barbara Rainey. *Moments Together for Couples: Devotional Handouts.* Manual ed. Ventura, Calif.: Gospel Light, Regal Books, 2000.

Richards, Clift, and Lloyd Hidebrand. *God's Special Promises to Me.* City: Tulsa: Victory House, 1996.

———. *Prayers that Prevail.* Tulsa: Victory House, 1990

———. *Prayers that Prevail for Your Children.* Tulsa: Victory House, 1994.

Sherrer, Quin, and Ruthanne Garlock. *How to Pray for Your Children.* Ventura, Calif.: Gospel Light, Regal Books, 1998.

## LIGHTHOUSE JOURNEY RESOURCES

Write, call, or e-mail HOPE Ministries to receive a catalog of Lighthouse materials that your family can use to supplement your journey. There are door hangers, posters, greeting cards with prayer messages, a Lighthouse decal to put in the window of your home, and many other wonderful resources. HOPE Ministries (Houses of Prayer Everywhere), 455 W. Springhill Ave., Terre Haute, IN 47802; (800) 217-5200; e-mail: linda@hope-ministries.org; Web site: www.hopeministries.org.

Lighthouse Movement for Kids: www.larrylighthouse.com

Lighthouse Movement: www.lighthousemovement.com

For Prayer-A-Grams, prayer poems, and many other prayer resources:

Harvest Prayer Ministries
Phone: (800) 217-5200
E-mail: hpm@harvestprayer.com
Web site: www.harvestprayer.com

PRAYER JOURNEY RESOURCES

# PRAYER MISSIONARIES RESOURCES

Children's Mission Resource Center—www.uscwm.org. Located within the larger Mission Resource Center, the Children's Mission Resource Center has everything you need and more to equip and challenge our next generation to join in the frontier missions movement. A regular newsletter, a list of books and materials, a lending library, mission education assistance, a quarterly newsletter, consultation services, and more are all available to help you direct your children or the children in your church to obey Jesus' command.

> Operation World Prayer Cards
> O.M. Literature
> PO Box 1047
> Waynesboro, GA 30830

Center For World Missions—www.cgpm.org. The Children's Global Prayer Movement, founded by Esther Ilnisky gives ways to involve children in being prayer missionaries.

> Esther Network International
> Esther Ilnisky
> Children's Global Prayer Movement
> 854 Conniston Rd
> West Palm Beach, FL 33405-2131
> Phone: (561) 832-6490
> Fax: (561) 832-8043
> E-mail: LCCIENI@aol.com

Mobilizing children to pray; prayer tools and other resources.

National Children's Prayer Network—www.childrensprayernet.org. Founded by Lin Story, this organization is a source of information on involving children in the prayer movement—also some good opportunities to pray globally!

www.calebproject.org—Lots of great resources (tools, books, videos, curriculums) for teaching kids to pray for the world.

*10/40 Window for Kids.* Video. Reignbridge. See Prayerwalking Resources.

T.H.U.M.B. Prayer Cards—Patterned after the T.H.U.M.B. acronym (Tribal, Hindu, Unreligious, Muslim, Buddhist), these cards help kids remember to pray for peoples without the gospel. Kids remember to pray when they see their thumbs or recall the religious group assigned to each finger! A leader's guide is included in each pack. A joint missions prayer project of Caleb Project and *PrayKids! Magazine,* the cards can be ordered from *Pray! Magazine* by calling 800-366-7788 or from Caleb Project (on the web at www.calebproject.org—go to their resources for kids section. Caleb Project has many resources for kids).

Adopt A Leader/People Group Info
   Reignbridge
   540 W. Highland Drive
   Camarillo, CA 93010
   http://reignbridge.com
   www.reignbridge.org

## PRAYERWALKING RESOURCES

WayMakers—Prayerwalk your zip code. Register and get materials from WayMakers. Also, use "Seek God for the City" materials for suggestions for prayerwalking opportunities during the Lenten season. This is a vital strategy for praying for your community. For these resources, contact the Web site www.waymakers.org.

Children's Prayer Congress—This event is sponsored by the National Children's Prayer Network (www.childrensprayernet.org). Mrs. Lin Story is the founder and director of this organization. For more information and a curriculum package (NCPN Brochure, Curriculum, Video Brochure, Decade of Prayer CD), contact ncpn2000@hotmail.com or by mail at National Children's Prayer Network, P. O. Box 9683, Washington, DC 20016.

*Prayerwalking for Kids*—a snappy, upbeat six-minute video for kids on how to pray for your community. This video can be ordered from

> Reignbridge
> 540 W. Highland Drive
> Camarillo, CA 93010
> http://reignbridge.com
> www.reignbridge.org

or by writing or calling

> Joey and Fawn Parish
> 540 W. Highland Drive
> Camarillo, CA 93010
> 805-987-0064

## OTHER WEB SITES AND MINISTRIES

www.harvestprayer.com—Harvest Prayer Ministries, founded by Dave and Kim Butts—articles and activities for parents, families, and kids on a wide range of prayer topics.

Lift Ticket Box—available from Prayer Point Press, 888-656-6067.

www.heritagebuilders.org—Many wonderful resources about prayer are to be found on this Web site. You will also learn how to develop your family's spiritual heritage. Check out the Family Night Guy!

www.ministrytotodayschild.com—This is a ministry of Pat Verbal, well-known author and speaker. Check out her resources, such as *Action Keys to Prayer: A Curriculum of Eight Reproducible Bible Studies.*

www.21stcenturykidsconnect.org—21st Century Kids Connect is a consortium of children's workers, parents, organizations, and Christian school teachers who believe this generation may well be the one that sees the Great Commission completed.

www.usprayercenter.org/family.html—The U.S. Prayer Center supplies articles and resources on prayer for families.

www.kidology.org

www.cherifuller.com—author and speaker Cheri Fuller. A wonderful resource for praying families.

Kids Pray!
  Children's Prayer Network of Australia
  PO Box 470 Hornsby
  NSO 2077
  Australia
  jmmackie@ozemail.com.au

Join a Prayer Kids Club—Elementary-age kids growing in Christ through prayer! There is a quarterly newsletter, and Prayer Notebooks and leader guides are also available.

  Prayer Kids Ministry
  47 Ravenwood Circle
  Bloomington, IL 61704
  309-662-0615
  Jan Merritt
  praykids@aol.com

Pray! Magazine—Parents, you can find many great resources in this outstanding magazine (www.navpress.com).

www.praykids.com—PrayKids! Magazine. From the publishers of Pray! Magazine, this publication is created to help children (ages 8–12) explore and grow in their understanding of foundational teachings about prayer. To learn more, get some great resources, or to download a sample issue, visit the Web site.

## ARTICLES BY KIM BUTTS

These articles can be read and printed for use in your family from the Web site www.heraldofhiscoming.org. They may also be requested by contacting Herald of His Coming, PO Box 279, Seelyville, IN 47878; Phone: 812-442-6200. The articles are listed below by date, for that is the easiest way to access them on the site.

| | |
|---|---|
| January 2002 | Teaching Your Children to Pray Grace-Filled Prayers |
| February 2002 | The Urgency of Raising Up a Praying Generation |
| March 2002 | Don't Forget What You Look Like! (Teaching Children to Obey the Word of God) |
| April 2002 | Praying God's Character into Your Children |
| May 2002 | From Fruitless to Fruitful (Teaching Children to Use God's Time Wisely) |
| June 2002 | Learning Spiritual Disciplines from God's Word (A Family Study of Psalm 119) |
| July 2002 | Restoring Revival Fire in the Family |
| August 2002 | Prayers of Forgiveness (Raising Merciful Children) |
| | |
| January 2001 | Practical Ways to Encourage Children to Pray |
| February 2001 | Preparing the Next Generation for Revival |
| April 2001 | Praying Scriptural Blessings into the Lives of Your Children |
| May 2001 | Prayers of Praise for the Family! |

| | |
|---|---|
| June 2001 | Prayer Evangelism for the Family! (Practical Ways to Fulfill the Great Commission at Home) |
| July 2001 | Raising Holy Children |
| August 2001 | The Transforming Power of God's Word in a Child's Life |
| September 2001 | Parent Prayer Warriors |
| October 2001 | Teaching Children to Trust in the Midst of Trials |
| November 2001 | The Family Fast (How to Develop the Spiritual Discipline of Fasting as a Family) |
| December 2001 | Prepare Our Hearts for the Coming of the Christ Child! (A Daily Prayer Calendar to Help Families Prepare for the Celebration of His Coming) |
| December 2000 | Teaching Children to Pray: Some Basics from the Scriptures |

MOODY
PUBLISHERS
THE NAME YOU CAN TRUST

DEMCO